BLACK SHEEP
WHITE LIES

TAMIKA DALTON

Black Sheep White Lies

Published by Tamika Dalton

Library of Congress Control Number: 2024925287

ISBNs:
Paperback: 979-8-9920855-0-1
Hardback: 979-8-9920855-1-8
E-book: 979-8-9920855-2-5
Audible: 979-8-9920855-3-2

Scripture References
Scripture quotations are taken from the Holy Bible, New Living Translation (NLT), copyright © 1996, 2004, 2015 by Tyndale House Foundation. Used by permission of Tyndale House Publishers, Inc., Carol Stream, Illinois 60188. All rights reserved. Scripture text accessed via BibleGateway.com.

This book is based on true events. Certain names, locations, and identifying details have been changed to protect the privacy of individuals. Any resemblance to persons living or deceased, beyond those specifically mentioned, is purely coincidental.

Printed in the United States of America.

"The smallest family will become a thousand people, and the tiniest group will become a mighty nation. At the right time, I, the LORD, will make it happen."

—Isaiah 60:22 (New Living Translation)

CONTENTS

CHAPTER ONE

What Lies Beneath 1
Struggling with countless insecurities, she's trapped in the very thing that will one day turn her into the same monster she has always hidden from.

CHAPTER TWO

The Last Shall Be First 9
In the unrelenting search for acceptance in a world that seems determined to cast her aside, the tables quickly begin to turn.

CHAPTER THREE

What's Yours Is Mine 17
Possession, pride, promiscuity, and the tangled web of love gone awry blur the boundaries of integrity.

CHAPTER FOUR

The Wages of Sin 23
Every action has a cost. The price of lies and lust begins to exact its toll.

CHAPTER FIVE

Checkmate **29**
A dangerous game of power and manipulation comes to a riveting point of no return.

CHAPTER SIX

A Match Made in Misery **33**
Two souls trapped in a toxic dance of love will soon become each other's greatest misery.

CHAPTER SEVEN

Seeing Double **37**
The struggle to reconcile two lives takes an unexpected turn, causing her to fall twice as hard.

CHAPTER EIGHT

Best Kept Secret **41**
The one thing she once desired so badly quickly turns into her most feared outcome.

CHAPTER NINE

The Great Escape **49**
Desperation sparks a bid for freedom, but fleeing the past proves harder than imagined.

CHAPTER TEN

If Walls Could Talk **57**
Within her home, every corner holds echoes of betrayal, leaving no space to hide from the pain.

CHAPTER ELEVEN

Shattering Vows
The sacred promises that once held their union together erupt into scandal, deception, and inconsolable pain.

CHAPTER TWELVE

Fatal Antidote
What once felt like a solution soon morphs into the very poison that could destroy her.

CHAPTER THIRTEEN

Nowhere to Hide
The ghosts of her choices and the truth she's avoided come crashing in with no escape in sight.

CHAPTER FOURTEEN

Snapped
The breaking point is reached in a moment of unrestrained fury, forever altering her path.

CHAPTER FIFTEEN

The Depths of Revenge
Consumed by vengeance, her calculated actions spiral into something much darker than she imagined.

CHAPTER SIXTEEN

Uncharted Territory
Stepping into an unforeseen life without a map, she's quickly confronted with something far more dangerous than her past.

CHAPTER SEVENTEEN

A Slave to Sin
Bound by the grip of temptation and the threat of her past intimate moments publicly surfacing, she frantically races to find a permanent solution.

CHAPTER EIGHTEEN

Prisoner of Perception
Shackled by the thoughts trapped in her mind, she fights to reclaim her identity on her own terms.

CHAPTER NINETEEN

What Doesn't Kill You
Her survival is a testament to resilience, each scar a symbol of a hard-won victory.

CHAPTER TWENTY

Redemption
In a final act of surrender and transformation, she finds the grace to forgive and the courage to live fully.

DEDICATION

I t is with heartfelt honor and deep humility that I dedicate this book to anyone who has ever lived in the shadows of disregard, endured the pain of isolation, or wrestled with brokenness, trauma, or addiction. Let these pages serve as a beacon of hope and undeniable proof that *God can*. There is nothing too massive, too overwhelming, or too far gone for Him. Every moment when it seemed like life was falling apart, God was there— gracefully and strategically weaving it all together for your ultimate good and His eternal glory.

To my husband, my mother, my stepfather Sai, my children, my sisters, my nephew, my grandmother, my brother Ennis, my godson Dedrick, my mentees—past, present, and future (especially the one who inspired this book)—and to every true friend who has honored our bond in both word and deed: I love you endlessly. Thank you for your love, strength, and unwavering presence in my story.

FOREWORD

Yes, yes, yes, Y-E-S! Tamika's story of transformation—from where she's been to where she is now—is nothing short of extraordinary. As I read *Black Sheep White Lies*—not once, but three times—I found myself profoundly moved, struggling to find the words to describe how deeply it touched me. This book is raw, real, and incredibly powerful. It is not just inspiring—it's life-changing.

Tamika's willingness to share her experiences with betrayal, false love, pain, and struggles is truly remarkable. Her honesty and vulnerability make it feel as though she is sitting across from you, sharing her heart. As I turned the pages, I could feel the weight of her journey and, at the same time, stand in awe of her incredible strength. Her candid admission of turning to addictive behaviors and worldly distractions to cope with life's challenges is so human and relatable—it reflects the struggles many face, but are often too afraid to admit. Writing a book about one's life—especially one filled with such turmoil and challenges—requires extraordinary bravery and honesty, and Tamika embodies both.

What stayed with me most, however, is her testimony of God's grace and mercy. Tamika's transformation is a beautiful and powerful reminder of how loving and transformative God can be. Reading about how He turned her pain into purpose brought tears to my eyes. Her story serves as a testament to resilience, redemption, and the boundless power of faith.

This book offers hope to anyone who feels lost, reminding them that God's love has the power to heal, restore, and redirect lives for His glory and purpose. It is impossible to read this book without being moved. Tamika's willingness to open her heart and share the depths of her journey is a gift to readers everywhere—a beacon of light showing that no matter how dark life may seem, God's grace is sufficient, and His purpose is always greater than our pain.

Black Sheep White Lies is more than a book—it's a ministry, a legacy, and a powerful tool for transformation. Tamika has stepped boldly into her calling, and the result is a work that will undoubtedly change lives for years to come. This book is a profound reminder that no matter where you are, there is always hope, healing, and a future filled with God's purpose and love. Bravo, Tamika, for shining your light so brightly and using your story to bring hope and transformation to others.

—Juanita Baker
CEO & Founder, *Beyond and Reflect*

INTRODUCTION

B etrayal cuts deeper when it comes from those you trust the most. Lies are louder when they echo in the chambers of your mind. And redemption—redemption demands more than you think you can give. But what happens when your darkest moments become the catalyst for your greatest transformation?

This is a story about pain, but it's also a story about power. It's a story about love's ability to heal, destroy, and resurrect. It's about the relentless pursuit of truth, even when every revelation threatens to break you. It's about forgiveness—of others, of yourself—and the unshakable grace of God that meets you in the ashes of your life.

For years, I was trapped in a vicious cycle of heartbreak, betrayal, and destructive choices. Every lie I told, every act of vengeance I plotted, every toxic relationship I clung to—it was all part of an intricate web I spun, believing I was in control. But the truth was, I was lost, caught in the grip of insecurities I tried to bury beneath power moves and misguided passion. I was searching for something—anything—to fill the void, not realizing I was looking in all the wrong places.

I loved deeply but chaotically. I fought for what I wanted but often destroyed what I needed in the process. My world was built on shaky foundations—promises I couldn't keep, trust I couldn't sustain, and love I couldn't fully grasp. And when those foundations inevitably crumbled, I blamed everyone but myself.

Then came the breaking point. The moment everything I had carefully constructed fell apart, and I was forced to confront the pieces of myself I had long avoided. Addiction whispered a tempting escape. Vengeance offered fleeting power. Shame tried to drown me. But in the depths of my despair, something stirred—a yearning for freedom, for healing, for a life beyond the lies.

This book is a testament to the journey I've walked—a journey marked by betrayal, brokenness, and the relentless grip of sin. It's also a testament to redemption, to the power of grace that transforms even the most shattered hearts. It's not a story of perfection; it's a story of progress. It's a story of learning to let go of the past to embrace the future God designed for me.

Through these pages, you'll find raw honesty, gripping moments of conflict, and the painful beauty of redemption. You'll see a woman fighting to reclaim her life, to repair the brokenness she caused and endured, and to uncover the truth beneath the lies she once clung to.

This book isn't just about me—it's about you, too. If you've ever felt trapped by your choices, betrayed by those you loved, or defined by your mistakes, know this: there is hope. There is healing. There is freedom waiting for you on the other side of surrender.

I share my story not as a perfect person but as a living testament that even the darkest pasts can lead to the brightest futures. My prayer is that this book will remind you that God is never far from your pain. He's there in the chaos, the heartbreak, the shame—quietly piecing it all together for your ultimate good and His glory. This is *Black Sheep, White Lies*. A story of loss, love, and the relentless pursuit of grace.

CHAPTER ONE

WHAT LIES BENEATH

You feel like everything is falling apart—right here, right now. Or maybe it already has. Your relationship? In shambles. Your finances? Hanging by a thread. Your emotions and mental state? A tangled mess. Even your spiritual foundation feels shattered, like it's slipping through your fingers.

You're buried under shame, suffocated by choices you regret, and haunted by failures that refuse to let you go. You wanted more—so much more. You dreamed of a life filled with purpose, love, and fulfillment. Instead, you're here—abandoned, judged, ridiculed. The tears that once poured freely are now gone, replaced by a hollow emptiness. It feels like the end, doesn't it?

Rock bottom isn't just a passing phase. It's a cold, unyielding reality that's taken up residence in your life. You've made it your home within your home—a place where the walls close in, and the weight of everything you've lost presses down harder each day.

And yet, you're here. It's why you're holding this book, staring at these words. Something drew you in—something you couldn't quite name but couldn't ignore. You felt it in the title, sensed it in the unspoken promise that this wasn't just another story. You recognized it as something real, something that saw you, even in your darkest place.

That connection? It wasn't random. It's not a coincidence. It's meant for you. Because our lives—our heartbreaks, our failures, our shattered pieces—are woven together in this moment. We've arrived here, at the same crossroads, searching for hope in all the wreckage.

This is where it begins. Right here. In the middle of the chaos, the brokenness, and the silence. This is where transformation takes root. Where redemption quietly unfolds.

And this? This is where your story starts again.

Me, I love a good success story—the kind where timelines flood with "I made it" captions, and families beam triumphantly in photos, like the journey was all sunshine and smooth sailing. Even strangers are celebrated. I often find myself cheering for people who will never notice my invisible confetti or the heartfelt "Congratulations" I'd sign at the bottom of their card. I cheer for them because I know what it feels like to have truly made it. I get it; I mean, everyone pretty much has their own celebratory moment of accomplishment at some point in life.

But what about the ones whose celebratory moments only arrive in their "Celebrating the Life of" captions plastered across the front of their obituary? The ones who don't make it, whose "finish line" arrives much sooner than their favored moment? Well, that someone was almost me.

I remember it like it was yesterday—or maybe it technically was. When you think about it, "now" is never an accurate time. The moment you get the word "now" off your lips, it's already later. There's never really a "now," but there's always a "then." And for most of us, our stories—our growth, our "then"—are so constant and ongoing that the battles we've fought against the tides of life, whether days, years, or decades ago, still feel like "just yesterday."

Growing up, I always felt "different" from everyone else. While I distinctly felt this dynamic at home, it became even more evident in spaces filled with people who didn't view me from an equal, independent perspective. It was as if I was forced into capacities with "normal" people, in "normal" atmospheres, yet I remained the black sheep. No matter where I went, I never fit in.

When I was surrounded by other Black people, I was always classified as "wanting to be white." (I still remember one particular childhood "friend" singing her dedicated solo: "I wanna beeeee white.") I was never the cool Black girl that all the other Black girls loved. On the flip side, whenever I removed myself from the cramped company of my own ethnicity, I was ridiculed for wanting to be whatever ethnicity matched the circle I was in.

Like, girl, relax—it's actually neither. If anything, at this point, I just wanted to be left alone. No sob story here, just facts. These facts are going to be super important later.

Yes, I grew up in a culturally diverse home. My mom is Black, and for many years, my stepdad was White, but we were never raised to view people through a color chart. Evidently, that perspective was isolated to my home. Let me be clear: this is not a book about race, nor is it about the racial profiling that truly happens within our own communities. This is simply a declaration—a piece of the puzzle—so you might better understand the conclusions others drew about me.

In truth, I probably was more well-spoken and articulate, and I can own that. But honestly, looking back now, I truly believe everything is spiritual. Sometimes people see something in you that you haven't even identified in yourself, and for many, that can be deeply intimidating.

I realize this struggle began early, but I distinctly remember my life starting in fifth grade. It's as if that's where all my real trauma began. As I crossed the threshold at Emerson Elementary, adversity anxiously awaited me. I was shy—shy and very plump. I wore an oversized, solid black T-shirt and baggy jeans. My natural hair was pulled into a ponytail. The cold weight of the long hallway set in immediately.

I remember another student approaching me, asking my age, and before I knew it, I blurted out, "Twelve!" Mind you, I was 11. In that moment, my brain jumped into survival mode, creating a way to leverage dominance by way of seniority. Since the looks weren't present, I needed something equally powerful: age. Of course, that little white lie didn't hold up for long, but it set the stage. This practice of telling "innocent lies" would co-write the pages of my life for years to come.

When in danger? Hide, lie, or both. This tactic became so common within me that I believed I was saving myself from the ill intentions of others. It became an autopilot defense mechanism.

I struggled a lot that year—and for many years after. My math teacher, Mr. Madrid, often joked and tried to lighten my stress, but it was to no avail. I was teased endlessly about my excessive weight and this dreadful scar I'd scratched into the center of my face—a souvenir from years of relentless allergies. I began to hate my life, school, and being the focal point of everyone's ridicule. And by "hated it," I mean I *HATED IT*.

Eventually, as time does, it passed. Before I knew it, I was headed into my first year of junior high. The only problem? The same people from elementary school were coming with me. I remember coming home countless times feeling trapped and unimportant.

My home life was becoming just as displeasurable. One day, I threw myself onto my bottom bunk, snuggled with my bright orange cat, Tiger, and bawled my eyes out. Of course, he just lay there, watching me with compassion—probably thinking, *How did I end up with this basket case?* In that moment, it felt like my cat was the only thing in the world offering me comfort.

I vividly recall entertaining, *I wonder what would happen if I just ran away.* So many times, I packed my clothes and hid them, even going so far as to practice opening my window quietly in the middle of the night. But every attempt failed—my confidence deserted me each time. Looking back now, I'm sure it was the prayers my mother constantly sent up, covering her children.

I was the middle child, and it always felt like I was important—until I wasn't. I didn't care about every parent in the world telling their children they love them equally. In my mind, in my soul, I felt alienated and unloved. My eldest sister seemed to mesh perfectly with my mother, and the baby of the family with my stepdad. I always felt like the only one who didn't belong—until it was time to go to my grandmother's house for the weekend.

There, I felt like royalty, and my siblings were the peasants. I say that jokingly now, but at the time, it couldn't have felt more real. In fact, that's probably why they always wanted to go back home so soon. Just as at home, she had her favorite—and it was me.

My grandmother and I were inseparable. My God, I loved that woman—in all her "rough around the edges" ways—with every fiber of my being. At the end of my eighth-grade year, my life finally began to change, or so I thought. For the better, I was sure. I was finally moving in with my granny.

As I settled into my new life, something unexpected started to happen: people began asking how I was losing weight. At first, I hadn't even noticed. I had been seriously overweight for as long as I could remember, and the idea of losing weight hadn't even seemed possible. But sure enough, I was. Not only was I shedding pounds, I was also able to wear makeup for the first time without any restrictions. That scar I hated? Concealed. Once and for all.

It felt like all my insecurities began to fade into the background, as effortlessly as brushstrokes sweeping across a blank canvas. My image was emerging!

For the first time in my life, I began to feel pretty. Not beautiful—just pretty. But that was enough for me. I loved it here. While my heart remained pure, humble, and compassionate, I couldn't help but revel in the fact that I felt pretty. And I wasn't the only one who noticed—so did others. Especially my grandmother.

I would catch her watching me as I walked past, her eyes warm with pride. Sometimes she'd come around the corner of the bathroom door as I was getting dressed and say, "Meka, don't you trust none of them girls at that school! If you get in a fight with any of them, they'll try to mess up your face cause they know it's pretty."

She'd immediately follow up with her signature tough-love warning: "And let me tell you something—I'll go to jail behind mine. I ain't gone do nothing but pass pills and make license plates. That's exactly what's gone happen if they touch you—now go get that red pepper and salt."

That was her way of telling me I looked nice. But believe me when I say I knew she meant every word. My grandmother was fierce, strong, wise, and unapologetically direct. She never bit her tongue or held back a thought. If she said I was pretty, that could only mean one thing: I was.

CHAPTER TWO

THE LAST SHALL BE FIRST

Before long, I was off to my freshman year of high school, and I was ready. More than ready. Not only was I headed to school, but I'd be pulling up there in a brand-new car. No license, mind you, but my grandmother, a nurse working long shifts and endless hours, trusted me with it. She'd taught me to drive and trusted me to do the right thing— not just with the car but in life. And for the most part, I kept my end of that unspoken bargain early on. She'd always been there for me, no limits, no questions. Letting her down was never an option.

Life was finally settling into something close to perfect. My mom and I had started to connect; we felt more like sisters, laughing and enjoying each other's company whenever we were together. And somehow, it seemed like everything about me was thriving. Transferring to a new school brought freedom from the people who had made middle school miserable; they'd drifted off, far from my world. And here I was, the new face on campus, even voted "Most Likely to Succeed." For the first time, I felt like God had heard my prayers. I thought I'd paid my dues, that the worst of life's trials were over. I couldn't have been more mistaken.

On my own little "Ideal Lane," I was balancing life—school, home, responsibilities. My grandmother was old-fashioned (a trait I appreciate more as I get older). I spent my days in class, keeping my grades up, and then came straight home to clean, cook full meals for her late shifts, press her uniforms, and keep up with the yard and myself. My social life was limited to phone calls, but somehow, it all flowed smoothly.

And, as it tends to happen, I developed a serious crush. My junior high crush became my first boyfriend during freshman year, and in my 15-year-old mind, he was a dream. I knew my family wouldn't approve, but I took a chance. He had that energy, that personality. Maybe it was because he was a little "hood" that he made me feel so safe, like my own personal security. Every girl likes to feel secure, right? After a while, I got the courage to bring him home. As soon as he left, my Granny let me have it.

"You really like him, don't you?" she asked.

"Yes ma'am," I replied, holding my breath.

She didn't hold her breath, nor did she hold her tongue. "Now you know good and well that boy is too black to mean you or anybody else any good."

"Granny!" I gasped.

She just chuckled, cutting her eyes at me. That was that. I knew she wasn't budging, but for now, that meant we were alright.

Not long after, Christmas rolled around, and I wanted to be the friend and girlfriend who had it all—and gave it all. I knew I couldn't ask my Granny for money to buy him gifts, so I made my way to Mervyn's (yes, that long ago) and tried stealing for the first time. On my way out, security caught me, and I found myself in juvenile detention for petty theft. I was crushed, not just for myself but for disappointing my grandmother. She was furious. And who did she blame? Yep, the company I was keeping. Sure enough, before long, that same boyfriend and some friends of his ended up stealing guns from our home. I was so humiliated, ashamed. That was it for us. Needless to say, building a future with him was not on my list of next moves nor preferences.

Time went on, and I started to form real bonds with three close friends: Uretha, Kendra, and Jen. In our own ways, we were all alike, like separate pairs of two peas in a pod. Kendra was quiet, sweet, and polite—still is, even today. Jen, on the other hand, had a spark, a vibrance that hasn't faded. Uretha was the true friend anyone would want by their side. Being around them felt good, different. Kendra and I spent most of our time together, but one day, Jen and Uretha were just... gone. No warning. I was crushed. This was my first experience of losing friends, especially friends I'd felt so close to.

Looking back, I realize that in adolescence, I had thought I had friends, but most were just people who kept me around to have someone to laugh at, someone they could joke about behind my back. Real friendship had been elusive, something I was only starting to understand.

One summer school afternoon, a girl I'd grown up with—a friend I'd held close—walked down the hall toward me. I waved, happy to see her, but she brushed past me with a loud snicker. Confused, I turned to see what I'd missed and realized she was walking with someone else, someone she clearly valued far more than me. My whole idea of friendship shattered in that instant. I could still hear the chatter and laughter behind me, my spirit sinking as I heard her say, "I don't really care." After all our years together, she was ashamed even to know me. I felt betrayed. But little did I know, one day the tables would turn—dramatically.

Life went on, and I began forging bonds with people who truly mattered. My brother Ricky, though not blood, became one of my favorite people, and Amber wasn't far behind. My grandmother would frequently have Amber over to help with her hair. Our families, especially our grandmothers, trusted each other, knowing that whenever we were together, we had each other's backs. Tikita was also a rock for me.

Soon, I wanted to work, to make my own money—especially after the theft incident. I started at a popular dine-in restaurant as a waitress and made good tips. For a moment, I felt like I'd arrived. But that feeling wouldn't last long. My unresolved pain and trauma were lurking, waiting to resurface.

When my big sister Tammy went off to college, I missed her more than I'd missed anyone. She was a Grambling Tiger, and no friendship could replace the bond we shared. When she returned from college, she moved in with my granny and me. They clashed sometimes, but she was an adult now and was rarely home.

My sister, like me, didn't have many friends, but she held those she did have close. I remember one of her friends making a very ugly, sly comment towards me. I didn't react in the moment, but I tucked the slight away and immediately disliked her. She reminded me of the adult version of everyone else who had hurt, embarrassed, or humiliated me over the years.

By then, I was working every evening after school, and I attracted attention—from men both young and older. I absorbed every ounce of it.

I'd spent years feeling small, ugly, and unnoticed. It felt like my turn, a chance to make up for all the times I'd felt invisible.

Eventually, I lost my virginity in a one-night stand. I was wrapped in shame, especially when my sister walked in right as he was leaving. She was furious, and her disappointment stung more than anything. But she didn't tell my grandmother—not that I knew of, anyway. I'd let her down, though, and it weighed on me. That's the danger of sin—it feels comfortable until you're lost in it, burning bridges without remorse.

My sister spent more time with her friends, and I found myself spending more time with my sister's friend's man. When my grandmother was out, I'd sneak boys—and eventually grown men—into her house. One night after work, Zay asked if I could take him home. He'd been flirting with me at work for ages, and this time, I gave in. I knew better—Zay was my sister's friend's boyfriend, at least ten years older, and way out of bounds. But I wanted to feel wanted, no matter how close to home that need led me. I didn't just want to feel wanted—I demanded retribution for the way she had insulted and offended me. This wasn't just about desire; it was about payback.

At sixteen, I wasn't running around with high school boys. The only people my age I'd been with were my ex-boyfriend and the one-night stand. The men I was drawn to, men older and seemingly unreachable, left me feeling validated. Now, at the big age of forty-two, I see how little it had to do with my appearance and how much more it represented my lack of self-worth. For them, I was just convenient. I became reckless, callous, and vindictive. I used one of the most sacred parts of myself as a weapon. I could have anyone, and I knew it. What I didn't realize was that I was letting anything have me.

I was quiet, sneaky, and discreet. At school, people saw me as the "untouchable, stuck-up pretty girl," but in reality, I was sneaking grown men, and later, upper-class guys from campus, into my grandmother's house. I felt nothing. Each day, I gave away a little more of myself.

At one point, I even entertained a substitute teacher who flirted with me at school. That came to an abrupt end when my Granny decided to randomly check my backpack, finding a note I'd written to him, planning to meet up off campus. That discovery was a disaster, but it didn't stop me. I was on a path of self-destruction, losing myself with every step. The more I participated in my own downfall, the less I cared. My actions weren't even about pleasure. They were about trading pieces of my soul, one by one, for something I couldn't even name.

After sleeping with Zay (on more occasions than I'd like to admit), I found myself repelled by him. He started to like me too much, clinging in ways I couldn't stand. The thrill was gone, and he was starting to feel like a nuisance. I realized that just as I'd detached from a healthy reality, I could detach from people—at least physically. Spiritually, though, I was tangled deeper than anyone could've imagined.

A few months later, I took on a job at a fast-food chain while balancing school and a few small modeling gigs. Academics came naturally for me; I excelled in everything except chemistry, which I still managed to pass. One night, as I took an order, the driver pulled up to the window, meeting my gaze with the biggest grin. He stumbled over his words, lining up the cheesiest pick-up lines I'd ever heard. I was in the "big leagues" by then— dating the local scene's most popular rapper, a man who spared no expense to impress me. So, with a casual smirk, I replied, "You cute, but I got a man." He took it as a challenge, but that's a story for later. That night, he drove away with his food and a side of rejection, but I knew this wouldn't be the last I'd see of him. Trust me, the enemy has nothing but time.

As the weeks since that summer school incident stretched on, so did the number of times Kennedy's kid's father, Lorenzo circled past my house— like a routine neither of us could break. One day, he finally mustered the courage to stop. I knew Lorenzo belonged to Kennedy and was more than aware of their children together. Perfect. Soon enough, we were on the phone for hours. He wasn't attractive, but this was personal. When my rapper boyfriend and I broke things off, Kennedy's man showed up right in time for me to get my lick back. Faster than I could even see coming, he would soon become my non-relationship/relationship. Ok, he was my sneaky link, but very present spiritual assignment.

My sister couldn't stand Lorenzo, and with good reason— Again, he was very grown and I was still very much-so a child in the eyes of the state of Texas. Despite Kennedy finding out, despite every conflict, I dealt with Lorenzo for years. I could not have cared less that she knew. I wanted her to, just like she wanted to make sure that the friend she conversed with about me knew that she "didn't really care". And yet, just like clockwork, I woke up one day and was over it. I cut him off, fell back and ignored his calls. My job was done. In my eyes, we had all got what we wanted.

As you might imagine, my focus on school soon slipped away. I was in constant fights, always caught up on the receiving end of the jealousy of other girls on campus, until I finally transferred to an alternative school, hoping to graduate early. My life felt like it was unraveling, stitch by stitch.

By this point, so many adverse events had occurred in my life that almost nothing moved me—but that was about to change. Right before turning 16, although never present, the only father that I'd ever known to be my father was hit by a car and died at the scene. As my mom came into my room, she had the worst look that any child could ever want to see on their mother's face. I'll never forget repeatedly asking, "What's wrong? What is it?" Her voice was soft but heavy with grief. "I'm so sorry, baby. Your father was killed today." My world crumbled. I was angry, broken, and numb. I could still hear his voice, as if he were in the room with me. "I love you," he would say softly. "Daddy gone send you some money, put your grandma on the phone."

In the days that followed, I searched for an escape, and that escape was music. I lost myself in the worlds that artists created, letting their songs take me anywhere but here, away from my own grim reality. But after he died, no matter how I tried, I couldn't shake the deep depression, anger, and sadness that took hold of me. I felt like I no longer belonged anywhere—not even at school. Dropping out felt like the only option, so I did exactly that.

Even though I was sexually active, I was mindful of my body, always protecting myself. But spiritually, I was in the most dangerously vulnerable place of all. I don't remember exactly how I convinced my grandmother to let me leave school, but somehow, I did. My Granny always had a trick up her sleeve. Not long after I dropped out, she called my older sister and me into her room. Her voice took on that commanding tone. "I called the college and got both of you enrolled in the Certified Nurse Aide program. You need a trade, something you can fall back on."

We exchanged a glance, silently agreeing, and replied with a simple, "Yes ma'am." Just like that, we were in classes, and before I knew it, we had passed the state exam.

CHAPTER THREE

WHAT'S YOURS IS MINE

I was 17 now, my sister was 20, and in our minds, we were "grown." Not long after, we decided to get our first apartment together. I was still doing small modeling gigs while we both worked full-time at a senior care facility. We loved working together, and for the most part, we loved living together.

We even planned our first trip: Spring Fest in Grambling, Louisiana, one of the biggest events of the year. My sister's old stomping grounds. There, I fit right in. The guys immediately started referring to us as the "fine girls from Texas". More reserved than usual, I eventually warmed up to one of my sister's close friends. Vell was a Cali boy, and he had the most pure, peaceful personality. Not to mention, our birthdays were 8 days apart. He was a Virgo, just like me. We meshed so easily…

There was something different about Vell—different from anyone I'd ever met. We spent the rest of our time at Spring Fest together, but we never slept together. I was ecstatic. How could I feel so connected to someone without sex? That connection captivated me. Over time, Vell and I stayed in touch, and a short while after, he came to Texas to spend a few days with me. For the first time, I felt genuine care in a relationship outside of family. Everything with him felt… authentic, like he might actually be my person.

But, being 17, patience wasn't my strength. Eventually, Vell left Grambling and returned to California, but we kept in touch, talking about our future and even some day marriage. Yet, the long-distance took a toll on me fast. Though I cared deeply for Vell, I was drawn to people who were here, in my "now." I had already felt alone for much of my life. Waiting felt unbearable.

Before long, I started entertaining the idea of settling for someone I could see daily. Little did I know this would lead to one of the worst mistakes of my life.

A few weeks later, I attended another modeling and talent event. When my contestant number echoed through the PA system, I took the stage, singing a song I'd practiced a million times. I don't remember the song, but whatever it was, it worked. I won that day. At the event's conclusion, a rapper who'd also performed approached me, inviting me to collaborate with him and his labelmates. I was thrilled that someone had finally noticed me for my talent, not just my looks.

I eagerly jotted down his contact info and agreed to visit the studio. In my mind, this was the big break I'd been waiting for. But looking back, it was setting the stage for a different kind of "break"—one that would leave me picking up the pieces for years to come.

A day or two later, I cleared my schedule, got super cute, and prepared to make a strong first impression. Every strand of hair was perfectly placed, lips lined, and confidence on 10. I was ready. Arriving at the studio in the next city over, I walked in, poised, pretty, and prepared. I strutted through the entrance, almost in perfect synchronicity with the blaring music in the distance, only to encounter a familiar face wearing a look of utter shock.

There, sitting at the table with a look of complete surprise, was the handsome, flirty guy from the drive-thru—the one I'd rejected. As I approached the table to introduce myself, he stopped me mid-sentence. "Nah, that's not your name. You too fine for that to be your name. You look like a VVS Diamond! From now on, you tell everybody they gotta call you Diamond. Tell 'em Savage said so!"

I was floored. My big, gullible self, blushing from ear to ear, replied, "Say less… Diamond it is, love."

We laughed, sharing the story of our first encounter at the drive-thru. It felt like fate had brought us here. Of all the people who could've been at that table, it was him. I stayed for hours, sharing my music. At one point, Savage asked, "You write your own music? You know how to count bars?"

"I write my own music, but what's a bar?" I asked.

Patiently, he explained the concept of musical timing, teaching me how to structure lyrics within a certain timeframe of a beat. The way he explained it ignited something in me. He was dominant and intriguing, with a look that reminded me of Ice Cube, just shorter. I'd always been a fan of Ice Cube, from his music to his movies. *Friday* had been my favorite movie for as long as I could remember, and I could quote every line as if I'd scripted it myself. The more I looked at him, the finer he got. Keep in mind, this was my 17-year-old mind at work.

As the night wore on, we flirted, talked, and I even met his young daughter. I know what you're thinking—there were more red flags than I could count. But in my adolescent mind, I brushed them all aside. And that wasn't even the worst of it.

Not only did he have a young child; he was married. Very… married. As if that wasn't reason enough to abort the entire mission, he also casually mentioned that he was 26. Yep, almost nine years my senior. But wait—it gets better. I later found out that the popular rapper boyfriend I had at the time Savage came through the drive-thru was none other than his most hated rival.

OMG, how is this even happening right now?

Imagine what I did to offset this whole circumstance in my mind? I immediately reverted back to how my ex had made me feel—the hurt I had buried but never really let go of came rushing back like an uninvited guest. That was my trigger point.

After everything he put me through, he deserved this. He deserved to feel every ounce of the pain he had caused me.

I felt compelled to shatter his peace. Even though we were no longer together, he still kept close tabs on me, always aware of what was happening in my life. I was certain this news would quickly find its way back to him.

Now I had a mission. And if you haven't figured it out yet, everything I was doing in my life up to this point was fueled by calculated intention. You hurt me; I destroy you. Very simple.

Seventeen quickly became the year my life spiraled. Savage and I were on the phone constantly—while he worked, while I worked, even from our separate homes. He spun the usual lines about being miserable in his marriage, only staying for his daughter. "We don't even have sex," he'd say. "I'm not attracted to her." He'd paint his wife as controlling, even claiming she'd tried to voodoo him by adding her menstrual blood into his spaghetti. Somewhere in the mess, I convinced myself I needed to "rescue" him, to free him from his misery. But in truth, he was leading me right into mine.

This was a dark moment—the perfect example of the phrase "the devil was in the details." I didn't recognize myself. Years of hurt had left me feeling entitled to do whatever I wanted, even if it meant wrecking someone else's life. I knew better. My family had judged me before, but this was an entirely new level of "Black Sheep Status." After a while, I stopped caring. Nothing mattered but what I wanted—I assumed that to be him.

CHAPTER FOUR

THE WAGES OF SIN

Things quickly became the unexpected. A feeling of power and pride overtook me. It was so strong; it surrounded me like impenetrable armor. I was afraid of no one and nothing: not his wife, her family, or even spiritual consequences. One day, without warning, I told him, "Give me the address." Thirty minutes later, I was parked outside his wife's house, ordering him to gather his belongings because he was leaving. Right now. Within moments, he walked out with his belongings and got in my car, leaving his wife and child behind.

Keep in mind, this occurred before sex was ever even a factor. Up to this point we still hadn't experienced one another sexually. Looking back now, Jezebel… is that you? It definitely was. Through leveraging my sexuality, trauma, and hurt that I'd endured in life, I had provided an open, welcoming door for anything that wanted to enter me spiritually.

I was reckless, rebellious and clearly overtaken by sin. At this point, I was so deeply submerged in my decisions, I felt I was way too far to turn around. So, I didn't.

That night, we arrived at the apartment I shared with my sister. I welcomed him with a long, warm embrace, showing him how much he needed me. I finally had my man. I knew he spent a lot of time in his own head—A LOT. I didn't want to leave any room for him to second-guess his decision. Knowing he had doubts, I wanted to erase any second thoughts. I'd already lied about my age, telling him I was 18. I needed him to be committed before he found out the truth. In my mind, everything was unfolding in my favor. As is clear, I had already been very sexually active, but as I stated prior, it was always just sex. Not this night. This night was different.

That night changed everything. For the first time, I felt my first real moment of sexual gratification, something beyond mere sex. I'd crossed a line, and now I felt as if any hope for redemption was beyond my reach. I was raised in church; my mother was a minister. I knew better than this. And yet, here I was, knee-deep in this new life, completely cut off from everything I'd been taught.

Soon after, we decided we needed a place of our own. We found an apartment and, just like that, I was playing house—cooking, cleaning, working, doing all the duties of a wife for another woman's husband. Divorce proceedings started, and I thought I had everything I'd ever wanted. This man was crazy about me, and very jealous, but in my own post trauma, and toxic headspace, I wanted it that way.

Not long before his divorce was finalized, I learned that I was pregnant. We were going to have our own family. I loved his daughter as if she were my own, but I couldn't wait to share our own child. Yet, as time went on, I could see the toll of not seeing his daughter weighing on him. He was frustrated, angry, sad. While I was certain he wanted me, I also knew how much he wanted the normalcy that came with having his daughter in his life.

Of course—and rightfully so, I suppose—his ex-wife did everything she could to stand in the way of him getting visitation. Honestly, I can't blame her. She was hurt, broken, and resentful. Who wouldn't be? I had completely disrupted the dynamic of her life, and then I had the nerve to be angry at her for making my man's life more complicated. Like, get real!

Looking back, she had every right to tell me to stay in a child's place. After all, that's exactly what I was—a child playing in a world far too grown for me. What I was doing was disgusting, but in that moment, I couldn't see it. While their marriage may have already been strained, it was still a marriage, and one day, I would pay for my decisions. Not just one day—many days, and in many ways.

In all the strength I thought I'd found, I couldn't have been farther from the truth. I was a disgrace. By this point, I was blazing right down the list of broken commandments.

Oh, but my time was coming—and it wasn't far off.

After enormous waves of relationship conflict, the unthinkable happened. I started having complications with my pregnancy—spotting and severe cramping. After visiting my OB/GYN, I was told that I needed to be on bed rest.

Several days later, while visiting friends I felt the sudden urgency to run to the bathroom for a frequent bladder release. Just as I began to squat, blood went everywhere. I knew I was losing my baby.

We rushed to the hospital, and when the doctor came in, I could see the sadness in his eyes. "I'm sorry, mama," he said gently. "You're having a miscarriage. We'll need to schedule a D&C immediately."

I was numb, filled with the gut-wrenching sense that this was some kind of punishment. Had my sins ultimately led to the death of my first child? Was this the price I was paying for the choices I'd made? I wondered if I'd ever be able to carry a child, if I'd unknowingly sacrificed my ability to bear children in my blindness.

The next day, Savage's ex-wife called him at work, falsely congratulating him on our "new child," knowing what we'd just lost. I hated her for it, but deep down, I knew I'd earned her bitterness.

Eventually, life resumed. I returned to work, and Sav and I continued our music. We had a seamless connection when it came to music, our creativity sparking together like nothing else.

Then, out of the blue, there was a knock on the door. By this time, I was pregnant again. Savage opened the door, and to our surprise, it was Dubb, a producer he'd worked with in the past. Dubb congratulated us, even mentioning that his girlfriend was also pregnant, due just four months before me.

After Dubb left, Sav stormed into the dining room, clearly upset. "How does he know where we live?" he demanded. I truthfully had no idea and said as much, but before I could even finish, he was in my face, yelling, so close I could feel the warmth of his anger and the spit from his words landing against my face. "I'll kill you and him!"

He snapped. His hands around my neck, he squeezed. I could almost feel the life draining from me, my vision fading. Just as suddenly, he let go. I timidly stumbled to the bathroom, the bruises already forming around my neck.

The following morning, leading with sexual embrace, he continued to apologize over and over. He was remorseful, I could feel it, and even if I was wrong... he felt good. In that moment, he began to ask me "you not gone leave me right"? "I gave up everything for you". "I gave up my daughter for you Meka". Lying there, I realized I'd lost more than I could ever imagine too.

Feeling guilty, I responded, "I know you're under a lot of stress, but you were wrong. Don't ever do that again as long as you live". He agreed.

We were good for a little minute after that incident, although periodically I began to see a side of anger from him that I would have never guessed existed. I mean literal unwrapped, unprovoked, timebomb rage.

I tried everything to pacify him. It felt like walking on eggshells, constantly watching for signs of his next outburst. One day, he'd be affectionate and caring, and the next, I'd be the target of his anger. Gradually, the violence intensified. What started as choking turned into full-blown physical fights. There were so many days I avoided my family, hiding bruises and scratches. My grandmother, mother, and sisters all grew concerned. My grandmother's warnings haunted me: "He'll start out choking you, then before you know it, you'll end up dead."

But I loved him. Why was he like this? I recall times where I'd run up thousands of dollars on my lines of credit to buy whatever he wanted. From studio equipment, to clothes, shoes, trips, you name it, I spent it. No matter what I did, he still was who he was.

There came a time where I was isolated from my friends and family and if it wasn't him, there wasn't much conversation. I lied to people who cared about me, little white lies, every day, so ashamed of the decisions I had made that led to my outcome. We went to church, he joined a ministry team, and the entire time this man was a monster behind closed doors.

While I feared him, I slowly began to hate him. Everything I had fought to build in life, I felt like he had taken from me. My youth, my credit, my confidence, my love, everything... I felt like he destroyed every single ounce of it, and I let him. Afterall, this was what I wanted right?

I started to feel something return in me that I had worked so hard to put out of my mind and out of my character. As the physical, verbal, and mental abuse continued, I grew smaller and smaller inside. I continued to cover my bruises at work and many times was so sore from fighting that I couldn't even assist my patients. I've always been very petite in stature and in all honesty, there are many men that weren't physically his equal. He made sure to remind me of that.

He made sure to let me know that no one else would ever want me and many times I even questioned my own womanhood. Domestic violence is so real. Even in writing, sharing these moments, years later, my tears still fall.

My children's father battled with many things, many which made me feel inadequate as a woman. I vividly recall asking questions about certain issues and being attacked to the point of fearing for my life.

Each time I thought I might have the strength to leave, I always found myself right back in the center of my misery.

CHAPTER FIVE

CHECKMATE

Finally, I'd had enough. One night, while at a studio session in Odessa, an argument broke out. Knowing him, I immediately tried to deescalate the situation, but that was too much like right. In front of a room full of people he slapped me with every drop of manhood he could muster up. That was it. That was my breaking point. I gathered my things and left. He, of course, went to his brother's house, his usual escape to avoid the police. He worked in corrections, and any charges would've jeopardized his career. I knew this, but at that moment, I didn't care. My desire for revenge ignited.

About an hour after the incident, I was at home when there was a knock at the door. It was one of his "big homies" who had been present at the studio during the incident. Yeah, okay. He asked if I was alright, then got right to the point: "Where's Savage?" I shrugged, telling him I didn't know and that he wasn't there. As I started to close the door, he held it open just a moment longer. "Diamond, let me go handle this, and I'll come back to check on you." I rolled my eyes, smirking slightly. "I'm good."

He gave me a look, "I know, but I'mma make sure you are. I know he be trippin'." I closed the door and went back upstairs.

Sure enough, just as my name is Tamika, that "good buddy" was back about 30 minutes later to check on his boy's fiancé. This time he wanted to come in, and I let him. As I walked upstairs, he followed. "Man, D, I been wanting you forever," he said. I knew it, too. I often saw glimpses of his lust for me. He was attractive, but I'd never thought of him as anything more than an acquaintance, especially given how close he was to my daughter's father.

But tonight, I ignored that line, purposely. Tired of being broken, I decided this was the moment I'd take my power back. It was about more than attraction—I wanted the power. While the sex was sub-average, it was the psychological shift that mattered. Everything was mental for me. I was actively and silently competing in chess. This move? Checkmate.

From that point forward, I decided to give him the same treatment he'd given me. Respect was gone, and love wasn't far behind.

By the time I turned 18, I'd had my first daughter, and life quickly became a financial struggle. I'm sure he'd argue differently, but I know I carried the weight of our household. He worked, sure, but every essential expense turned into an argument, every dollar met with complaints. Eventually, we moved into a decent home owned by one of his "older lady friends"— a strange setup, but I tried to let it go. Rent was $2,800 a month, and by that time I was the only one working, while he stayed home, playing PlayStation, producing music, and "watching" our daughter.

It didn't take long for tensions to flare up again. This time, I didn't hold back. I had nothing left to lose; whatever he was on, I would match it, times ten. I was done playing nice. By this point I was venomous.

I went through the motions, numbed by constant stress. To get by, I borrowed money from a coworker whose check would end up bouncing. As a result, I in turn ended up writing probably over fifty bad checks, which also bounced one after another. Soon, detectives were knocking, warrants were issued, and two counties fully intended to prosecute. I was in and out of jail so often it felt surreal, with each missed payment leading to new warrants, charges, and fines that more than tripled my original debt. Did he try to help? Not once.

That period made me the official "black sheep" of the family. My sisters were upstanding, law- abiding citizens without so much as a traffic ticket, while I had my face plastered in the Crime Stoppers paper. August 15, 2002, I celebrated my baby's first early birthday, knowing I'd be reporting for a 30-day jail sentence the next day. Missing her official birthday was a kind of pain I hadn't known existed. This situation would cause me to view him in an even less respected light.

Of all the things starting to come full circle for me, the one thing I hadn't yet realized was that this very circumstance—heartbreaking as it was—was the quiet beginning of God's plan and a redirection for my life.

CHAPTER SIX

A MATCH MADE IN MISERY

When I was finally released, the prosecutors offered a deal: plead guilty to a felony, take five years of probation, pay $5,000 in two days, plus $400 monthly. Otherwise, it was state jail time. I was at a complete loss. My court-appointed attorney didn't inspire much hope, and I felt as if my life was slipping through my fingers.

I prayed harder than ever, knowing my family couldn't help. Then, like an answered prayer, my stepfather Sai stepped in. He didn't have to, but he believed in me. He pulled from his 401(k) to cover what I needed, even facing penalties to make it happen. His kindness saved me from prison, and to this day, I'd do anything for him.

As we entered 2003, I finally felt a flicker of peace, knowing the cycle of warrants and fines was over. I prayed often, realizing my hardships weren't just karma—they were the seeds I'd sown. I was ready to change.

On Valentine's Day 2003, despite it all, we got married. I wasn't ready to give up, and I wanted to rebuild my life with some sense of stability. Shortly after, I learned I was pregnant again. I was hopeful but cautious, wanting a better experience than my last two traumatic pregnancies. They had both been filled with loss and violence. But soon, old fears began to reappear, like shadows from a nightmare I couldn't shake.

My marriage began to fracture, until one night, after another argument, he packed his things and left, as he often did. This time, I didn't try to stop him. I felt defeated, sitting alone after putting my daughter to bed, I became consumed with a sense of failure.

I didn't want to continue this cycle. This was it—my moment of surrender. I took myself into the closet, closing the door behind me, not to surrender to God, but to surrender to an ending. My daughter deserved a better mother. My family deserved peace, free from the constant worry I brought them. In my mind, I was a complete failure. Sure, I'd earned my GED, but in comparison to my siblings' achievements, it felt meaningless. Yeah, they say comparison is the thief of joy, but at this point, living itself felt like the thief of mine.

As everything collapsed around me, I was ready. I picked up my loaded pistol, and my thoughts began to race. I sat there a moment, one thought cutting through the noise: *Who's going to find me like this?*

What if my daughter woke up and came looking for me before her dad got home? The thought was paralyzing. I could see her opening the closet door, finding my lifeless body in a pool of blood—a sight that would scar her forever. And what about my unborn child? She hadn't even had a chance at life. I sat there, wrestling with the weight of it all, while memories of my grandmother, my mother, and my siblings crowded my mind. *What kind of coward am I?*

I stared into the barrel of the gun, longing for an escape. This couldn't be the life I'd chosen—yet, it was. After what felt like hours, I finally forced myself off the closet floor and returned the gun to its rightful place. A wave of anger washed over me, furious that I hadn't taken my exit. *How do you even fail at dying?*

A day or so passed before my husband returned. I kept my distance, wrapping myself in silence and isolation. I didn't want him near me. I blamed him for the mess that was my life, but in reality, I knew the truth: the person responsible was the one I saw in the mirror. The pretty girl who'd finally surfaced after years of hiding, yet was rotting on the inside. The girl who carried hurt, anxiety, bitterness, and unforgiveness like prized trophies. A liar, a thief, an adulteress, a fornicator, an idolater, a promiscuous prisoner—all bottled up, held so tightly shut that no force could pry her open.

Days turned to months, and December came. I welcomed my second beautiful baby girl into the world. Looking into her eyes, I felt it was all worth it. How had these perfect petals of life grown from a dying plant? These perfect little souls had emerged from what felt like a dying, broken life. That could only mean one thing: it wasn't the plant that was dead—it was the water feeding it that was contaminated.

Before long, we both realized we were only bandaging a critical wound. He made it clear he wasn't ready to let me go, but emotionally, I had already left long before. Our relationship deteriorated into constant fighting, and eventually, he cheated on me with a stripper. I knew. I was numb. In a way, it felt like the final excuse I'd been waiting for, a reason to solidify my escape.

Ironically, I stayed calm, back in my mental war zone. The vengeful, narcissistic part of me was ready to end it on the grounds of his betrayal, even though truthfully told, I'd done plenty of dirt myself. I'd never lived up to the Proverbs 31 blueprint, but now I had no desire to. With calm resolve, I stepped into my "love 'em and leave 'em" phase, more intentional than ever. Without a single drop of sweat from my brow, the old me was coming back—more vengeful, more hateful, and more calculated than before.

CHAPTER SEVEN

SEEING DOUBLE

When the time was finally right, I disclosed my plans. I'd been quietly arranging my life to move to Houston, determined that nothing would stand in my way. I was still writing and performing secular music and wanted to be in a place where I could thrive. But when I told him, for the first time, I saw him crumble. His face shattered, and all the hurt he'd caused me seemed to reflect back onto him in that moment. I'd planned to make him pay for the trauma he'd put me through, but seeing his pain caught me off guard, freezing me like a deer in headlights. Seeing him hurt, hurt me. Somehow, I'd never factored in that moment.

I couldn't bring myself to leave him alone, just like that. I knew, in his own twisted way, he needed me. I started second-guessing, revisiting my decision over and over. Finally, against my better judgment, I invited him to join me. He accepted, of course. In a toxic way, I knew I held something over him, a power he couldn't shake. I fed that dynamic, knowing how much he desired me, knowing his world revolved around me, even when his actions betrayed that. No arrogance—it's simply the truth.

So, we moved to Houston together. I convinced my mom to keep the girls while I got settled. My life was still chaotic, and I think my mom sensed that. She wanted her grandchildren to be safe, even if that meant protecting them from me. My daughters thrived in her care, and they loved their Nana.

My oldest sister, though, was livid that I'd left the girls with our mom. Every time we spoke, she reminded me of her disapproval, urging me to "woman up" and take responsibility. Her words always turned into a catalyst for discord, but deep down, I knew she was right. Of course, I didn't want to hear it.

Meanwhile, he and I settled into a nice apartment—one I couldn't really afford. My car payments, still in my grandmother's name, were past due. I was building up more bills than I could handle, yet living as if I had it together. It was giving "high-end bum" vibes at its best.

Desperate for distraction, we booked a studio session with some guys we'd met at an event. Priorities were out of place as usual. Once we were there, I could tell he was uncomfortable, something about it made him uneasy. But when we got home, that unease boiled over into an argument. I hate to say it, but for once, his suspicions had some merit.

There was a man at the studio who was absolutely gorgeous—literally one of the most attractive men I'd ever seen. Sav knew it, and it triggered something in him. The argument escalated, and leaded to him pulling a butcher knife on me. I knew, without a doubt, that he was serious. For over an hour, he raged, issuing threats. With our kids safely at my mother's, it was as if he felt no boundaries.

Finally, he calmed down, and as he did, I delivered my final speech. "Sav, this is not going to work. I deserve better, and so do you." He sat in silence as I told him it was time to pack up and go back to Midland. I think he was exhausted, too. Either way, I was done allowing him to control me or my happiness. I had not moved this far away from home to allow his dysfunction to follow.

Two days later, he left. I sat alone in that apartment, trying to wrap my mind around it, wondering if this was truly real. It was finally over, the cycle grinding to an end. I wanted him to be free, but even more than that, I wanted to be free.

Just as Sav had predicted, I eventually found myself back at the studio—this time alone. My defaulted nature kicked back in, the old patterns surfacing. I knew that if I wanted someone, I could have them, and this time was no different.

In no time, we became an item. I was completely intertwined with him and his family. This time, I felt something truly different. He was a twin, brilliant and gorgeous, with a quiet, reserved demeanor that hid just enough of a "street mentality" to keep things interesting. He did everything for me, effortlessly. There was something about him that I couldn't shake.

While still technically married to my ex, I continued to date him. Everything on the surface seemed perfect, yet spiritually, I felt more and more disconnected from God. I had a pattern: I would build something, then destroy it. I'd connect, then reject. It was as if I couldn't accept being loved properly, even though he met me exactly where I was, time and time again.

I could tell I brought something out in him too, challenging him to be better, to want more from life. I had this ironic nurturing effect on people, yet I couldn't find a way to nurture and grow myself. We shared a close, almost unbreakable bond, but I was haunted by the feeling that something was always missing. How could I draw in everyone I wanted, make them crazy about me, only to search for a way to sever the ties once I had what I thought I wanted?

Then one day, it hit me like a ton of bricks: *I'm damaged goods.* I was like a storm, a brewing tornado that destroyed everything in its path. I lived for toxicity, for the chaos of make-up and break-up. I craved it.

Eventually, I started to settle down. My children came to live with me, and they loved "Twin." He didn't have children of his own at this time, but he'd come from a nurturing, loving family and it showed. He was everything the girls and I needed, yet I couldn't fully commit. Twin gave me a sense of peace and security that allowed me to operate in my femininity. I had finally found something good, but as soon as I saw his one flaw, a choice he'd made in life that didn't sit well with me, I latched onto it and wouldn't let go. I gave him an ultimatum, knowing it was impossible for him to meet it. He fought for me, tried to make things work, but I rejected him.

While there was one life decision he was making that I refused to accept, discord was all I knew. When things felt right, they felt too right. I was so accustomed to dysfunction that stability and healthy relationships made me uneasy. I was broken, carrying the weight of all my unresolved pain. No matter where I went, there I was, always with myself.

I demanded better but didn't feel I deserved it, and once I had it, I was uncomfortable. I didn't miss Sav, but his words haunted me. The things he'd said to tear me down echoed in my mind long after the physical scars had healed. Years of verbal abuse loomed over me like a dark cloud. My spirit was fractured, venomous, and I had truly lost myself, cut off from anything that could lead to my healing.

CHAPTER EIGHT

BEST KEPT SECRET

As Hurricane Katrina approached, I found myself homesick and wanting to be close to family. I told T I was heading back to West Texas. Once again, I hurt someone who didn't deserve it, driven by my own restless desires. I packed up my life in Houston, spent a little time with him, and invited him to come along, knowing deep down that he wouldn't leave the city he loved for Midland. He promised he'd visit, and he did. Every time I flew through Houston, he was there without fail, meeting me at the airport and wrapping me in his arms as if no time had passed.

He loved me—I could feel it—but I just couldn't process it.

Back home, life was the same: oil fields, tumbleweeds, and not much else. Eventually, I started dating again, even though I knew it was too soon. I got involved with someone, though there was no real connection. We were just two liars lying to one another, passing time, filling empty spaces.

I'd involved myself with someone, really that I had no general interest in. He truly wasn't my type, but there was that "something" about me that made every man I dealt with cling to me. I mean to the point of stalking me, breaking in my home and calling me from my home phone, destroying my vehicles… yeah, that type.

I think I lived for the thrill of it all. I mean, what woman doesn't want a man that's absolutely obsessed with her? As I've said countless times, it was deeply spiritual—I knew that—but somehow, the chaos fueled a part of me I couldn't seem to unclench.

Towards the end of our "relationship"—if you could even call it that—I was back in full revenge mode, mentally logging every one of his mistakes, waiting for the moment I'd get my lick back.

One day, I ran into Dubb at the grocery store—the same Dubb who'd set off that infamous spiral with the girls' dad. Our interaction was brief. He gave me his number, telling me to hit him up if I needed work done on my album. Not only had Dubb known my children's father, he had also produced, almost exclusively for Money, my rapper ex-boyfriend from years prior. That night, I mentioned him to my neighbors, Tay and Brandy, and we all gushed at the mention of him, marveling over how "fine" he was. Dubb was a unique type—like a super-hybrid soulful white guy, the kind who was effortlessly cool, laid-back, and seemed born with that "it" factor. To this day, we still call him "Jon B."

Meanwhile, back in reality, my life was a mess. I was still legally married to the girls' dad, still had feelings for Twin, was wrapped up in a dysfunctional fling, and now, Dubb had entered the picture. I know it sounds like chaos, and truly it was. But here's the caveat: if I share my story—you see God's glory.

I was still heavily involved in music, working on a new album, and in need of production. After the "Dubb encounter," I reached out, asking if he could send me some tracks that matched my style. He suggested I come over and have a listening session, offering to create something custom for my project. The idea of working together was exciting.

By this point, my fling was at its end, but I wanted to level the playing field before I made my exit. That evening, I told him I had a studio session, which he accepted without question as he was headed to a poker tournament. I asked to borrow his truck since my car was in the shop, and he agreed, unwittingly giving me the perfect setup.

I drove his truck over to Dubb's house, and when I arrived, he noticed right away. "Your boyfriend let you drive his truck?" he smirked, clearly picking up on the situation. I played it off with a laugh, "Boy, stop—that's my brother's truck. I don't have a man." Just lying, as usual, adding layers to the complicated web I was weaving.

Like… what brother??? The "not having a man" part was sort of true, sort of not. We were literally at our end—he probably wouldn't have agreed, but for sure, we were done. What I was certain about, though, was how liberated I felt, sitting in his truck parked outside another man's house. Especially after all of the disrespectful stunts he'd pulled. And this was just the beginning.

Naturally, the conversation shifted to our relationship statuses. I slyly asked, "So, where's your girl? Did you tell her *the* Diamond was coming over?" I knew women were aware that I was highly sought after, and they almost always hated the idea of their man being around me. Ironically enough, I never wanted the ones women were unnecessarily pressed about, but I was a threat. They knew it, and I knew it. Dubb quickly responded, "I'm single. Me and my ex? We've been over—I kicked her out like two weeks ago." I raised an eyebrow, giving him a skeptical look. "Mmmmhmmm." He laughed, unfazed. "No, seriously. Let me give you a tour of my house. Ain't no woman here. It's just me and my son."

I agreed and rose to follow him through the house. And sure enough, it was a classic bachelor's setup—bathroom, bedrooms, living room, and kitchen, all with that "bachelor" feel. It wasn't tidy, which led me to believe a woman hadn't been around. Either that, or she didn't believe in keeping a clean house. Whichever it was, I noted it. In my mind, where there's lack, there's need, and I love a clean house. My OCD was already making a mental checklist of all the things I'd fix. (Yes, that's how my brain works.)

While the house was free from any sign of a woman's presence, I did happen to notice a green picture frame on his dresser. As I approached it, he blurted out, "That's old!" I replied, "That's fine. I still wanna see it." He didn't contest.

As I picked up the frame, I saw it was a picture of him and *her*. Before I could stop myself, the words spilled out. "Boooooy… this is her? This is your ex?" I shook my head. "I know you're lying! How did she pull you?" My cocky arrogance came through boldly. He laughed, giving me the green light to keep going. "Baby, she is ugly!" How dare I, right? This was coming from the same person who'd walked through life with a filthy spirit and, for years, saw herself as ugly. He shrugged and said, "Man, I don't even know." I just had to get the last word in: "I know you don't. I *knoooow* you don't." We both laughed as we headed back to the production room.

Finally, I was ready for "what I'd come for." He started playing tracks from his catalog, and you could hear the soul in every single one of them. I loved them. "What you charging me?" I asked. His reply made it clear this was going in exactly the direction I'd hoped: "For you, we'll work something out." I gave a cute, feminine snicker. "That works."

As he continued to play the instrumentals, my thoughts became louder than the music. I watched him, my eyes traveling from head to toe as curiosity sparked. *He is so sexy. What color are his eyes? Green? Hazel? I bet even he doesn't know.* Everything about this man captured me—his demeanor, his conversation, his confidence, his fatherhood, his style, and, of course, his music. After all, that's what had brought us together in the first place. Y'all, *he was IT!* He was intoxicating, and instantly became my every want.

I'd "wanted" people before, but this was different. In the past, I wanted them for some schemed, manipulative purpose—never anything long-term. But with him, I felt something different. I could actually see myself with him. And mind you, I'd never dated a white guy. Sure, I'd had a crush years ago, but it was more of a friendship. This felt like it could go so far beyond anything I'd ever known. I didn't know how or when, but I knew. I just knew.

As the evening drew to an end, we started to wrap things up and headed outside toward my "brother's truck." I had to get home to the girls, and he had to pick up his son from his parents. Approaching the street, I couldn't help admiring his beautiful black sports car—it was clear he'd put a lot of love and money into it. I walked over for a closer look, and he followed. As I turned around to compliment his prized possession, he was standing right in front of me. Before I could say anything, he stopped me.

"When am I gonna see you again?" O-M-G… it was happening! I didn't know why I was caught so off guard—I'd always gotten who I wanted—but this was different. I knew this caliber was out of my chamber. Overcome with excitement, I tried to play it cool. No way was I letting him see me geek out. This was everything I'd been hoping for.

I casually replied, "I don't know. We'll see."

"When do you wanna see me?" He was so polished and self-assured as he effortlessly replied, "Every day." *WHAT?* Who says that? I'll tell you who: a man who knows what he wants and exactly how to get it. And oh, he could definitely get it.

I knew I was blushing. My face felt flushed, and I could feel it. I fought to keep my composure, but he kept disarming me. "Let me take you out," he said. In my mind, I was thinking, *Take me out? You can do more than that. Take me off the market FOREVER. Take me captive… JUST TAKE ME!*

As I melted into a vulnerable pool of excitement, I pulled myself together, shoulders back, finally finding my words. "I can do that. Let me rearrange my week, and I'll put you at the top of it." *Girl, there you go! Act like you've done this before!* Whew… that was such a close call. I definitely needed to regroup.

Desperately needing to reclaim my composure, I started heading to the truck, but he stopped me one last time. He leaned in gently to kiss me, and every single guard I had came crashing down. I returned the kiss, knowing in that moment it would change my life forever.

As I got into the truck, my thoughts kicked into overdrive. *What just happened?* I assure you, music was the last thing on my mind—total understatement. I realized right then and there that whatever "thing" I was in couldn't continue. I needed to end it, and I needed to do it now.

CHAPTER NINE

THE GREAT ESCAPE

When I got home, the guy I was involved with almost instinctively asked, "How'd it go?"

"Ummm, it was good." I could tell he sensed something was up.

"Good... that's it?"

"Yeah, that's it."

Since he was naturally sneaky, he could easily spot my deceit. "Tamika, what's up?" Of course, I downplayed it and hurried to deflect the spotlight off myself. "How was your tournament? I see you're home early... that's new."

"Yeah, I am. Had to get home to see what you're up to."

"Boy, don't start. In case you forgot, I'm not the one who comes up missing for hours at a time. I'm always accounted for—so do you really want to do that tonight?"

He sat there for a moment, clearly debating his options. I could see he wanted to pry, but his own track record made him hesitant to fully commit to the interrogation.

"Yeah, I thought so." I always had to have the last word, and it always had to be something slick.

I treaded lightly, though; this was the same man who had smashed my Cadillac with a baseball bat because my ex came over to see the kids.

"Aren't you tired of doing this yet?" I knew he wouldn't agree to let me go willingly, but I had to convince him to… and quickly.

That night we went to bed, but I could hardly sleep, thinking about Dubb. I needed help. The next day, I called a trusted ally, knowing if anyone could help me out of this mess, it was going to be her.

When I finally got a moment alone, I called her. "Giiiiiiiiiirrrrlllllll… you won't believe this."

"What!!??? What you done did?" You'd have to know her to understand her reaction, but let me tell you, she was super funny and super silly. We burst into laughter.

As I spilled all the details, even she was speechless, unsure of how to help. "Let me think of something," she said, laughing in her usual goofy way. I reminded her of the urgency. She impulsively interjected, sounding like somebody's granny, "Alright… but you know he's crazy."

"I know! That's why I need your help!"

In what seemed like no time, we accomplished the mission. My fling was back at his apartment, and I was rapidly weaning him off of me. I stopped answering calls or replying to texts. I refused to let anything jeopardize what I knew I wanted.

Once the dust settled, I finally invited Dubb over. We'd talked every day since our first encounter, warming up to each other fast. I couldn't wait to have him visit me, and I knew my neighbors would celebrate this "victory" right along with me.

While Dubb was a perfect gentleman, he still had some lingering "playa" traits I knew I'd have to help him grow out of, but guessed it wouldn't hurt to try.

Finally, the time came to open my doors to him. Anyone who knows me personally knows I love to cook, and I'm quite seasoned at it. Cooking is my love language, and it would later evolve into a career as a chef.

My grandmother always used to say, "If you want to keep a man, you better know how to cook. Don't no man want no slouchy woman," and she was right.

So, I put her theory into motion, making an elaborate first meal for Dubb—the first of many—and he loved it. Although he didn't bring his son that time, he got to meet my daughters, and they connected instantly. Despite my crazy life, I'd always been very selective about who I chose to allow around my children.

I watched him interact with the girls and saw their responses, and I could hardly believe it—it was magical. Everything was pure perfection.

Not long after, Dubb called to tell me his son had broken his arm and needed to go to Lubbock for care. I immediately offered to go with him, and he accepted.

Dubb had been a single parent for his son's entire life. His son's mother was completely absent, and he had never known the presence of a mother figure.

I dropped everything to make the trip, knowing this bonding time was much needed.

A few days after we returned from Lubbock, Dubb invited me on a weekend trip to Arlington to spend time with his son and extended family. He had tickets to a Rangers game and wanted me to be there. Unfortunately, due to the short notice, I couldn't attend, but I wanted to go badly.

We talked the whole time he was away, and I missed him. He and his son were growing on me fast. Keep in mind, this was the same son Dubb had mentioned that he was expecting during that visit to my ex's apartment almost four years prior. It's funny how life can circle back around.

Our children enjoyed each other so much, acting like they'd been born siblings. The two oldest were only four months apart and did everything together. My youngest daughter wasn't yet two, so she definitely kept the two older kids on their toes.

Our blended family felt like a perfect fit, and I was the happiest I'd ever been. I felt safe. Everything I'd ever wanted in a man, Dubb was. I trusted him.

It was as if all the viciousness that had once defined me slowly released its grip on my life. I could finally be myself. I began to love from a pure place, and, for the first time, I allowed myself to truly receive love.

Then, just as quickly as everything had become perfect, it all came crashing down, and the foundation of our relationship shattered.

After adding a line to my phone account, his ex-girlfriend reached out to me. She told me that Dubb was still calling her (from my phone, at that) and claimed he'd made some derogatory comments about me when she'd asked him about me months before he and I had even crossed paths. I found it interesting that she'd felt the need to bring me up, worrying whether he was interested in me before I was ever even a thought in his mind. It reminded me that even when I didn't realize I was a threat to someone, I still was—and they could see it.

Nevertheless, I was beyond furious—furious and hurt. Some of the things she claimed he'd said about me instantly stirred up old emotions I thought I'd left behind. I wanted so badly to pour myself into him and our relationship, but the old me showed right back up. But this time, I was different.

Armed with all the details, I confronted him; and as expected, he lied.

I'd always had this pet peeve about lying. It set off something in me. The irony that I'd lied to so many people yet raged about someone lying to me? Complete craziness.

But it was fine. Lie or truth, I had already decided I was done. I'd come too far to let him or anyone else set me back. I didn't care how much I liked him.

The crazy part was, hearing from her didn't spark a bit of insecurity in me. If anything, I knew what I had to offer—and she simply didn't compare. She couldn't cook, didn't clean, and the list went on. She couldn't hold a candle to me on my darkest days. She was basic, at best.

Nonetheless, if he did want her, I wanted him to have her.

After calmly making my point, I dismissed him, saying, "Play with somebody else." I had him drop my phone off and cut him off completely, without a second thought.

I began to carry myself with a new class. Still very intentional about my moves, I started to approach life from a different perspective.

For weeks, he called. I ignored most of his attempts, but occasionally I'd answer, just enough to leave a mark in his mind. By this point, I was a master of mental chess.

Soon, even his mother started calling me. While I'd talk to her, I refused to budge. Day after day, I heard about how much she disliked his ex. I felt bad for her, but it was what it was.

At this point, I thought, *Y'all are making y'all's problems, my problems.*

After about three weeks of cat and mouse, I finally agreed to go to a movie with him. Geez, let's just get it over with. I'd deliberately made him work for that date. I decided not to be accessible or available, encouraging him to spend time with anyone he still felt the need to entertain—because I certainly intended to do the same.

When the day of the movie finally came, I went the extra mile with my appearance—heavy on the "extra."

I looked flawless—not to attract him, as he was already drawn to me. This was more about repelling him while looking stunning doing it. My masterful mind was fully engaged, and soon, I would be too.

As we approached his car, I waited for him to open my door. No lie, this man had something up his sleeve that I could have never prepared myself for.

I turned around, and my eyes were immediately drawn to his stance. *He was on one knee!*

WHAT IN THE ENTIRE WORLD WAS HAPPENING RIGHT NOW?

I felt faint. "Wait... what? Are you serious right now?" He was, indeed.

The words that followed drew me in like nothing I'd ever heard. It felt like I'd truly met my match—witty, calculated, and overflowing with the element of surprise and charm. He was indeed, the male version of me.

At the end of his perfectly executed speech, he finished with, "Will you marry me?"

Before I could gather my thoughts or slow down my words, I'd accepted.

What was I doing? Now I was engaged! Engaged and still technically married. *Lord Jesus, it's me again.*

Within days of accepting his proposal, Dubb made sure I knew he wanted our new family all under one roof.

I thought to myself, *He's trying to make sure I don't involve myself in any other commitments.* Ironically, I could tell he sensed my patterns, as if he could read my mind.

He worked tirelessly to fill any space I might be tempted to fill elsewhere due to his initial slip-ups. And he was on the right track.

In what felt like no time, we were packing up my house and moving into one home. Our children were thrilled to be together every day, as if we all just flowed effortlessly into our new life.

Just as quickly as the engagement had started, before I knew it, our wedding day was upon us. After a pending divorce from my first husband had dragged on for what felt like a lifetime, it seemed like an act of God when it was finalized just in time for my wedding.

Thank you, Jesus! And just like that, I was Mrs. Dalton.

CHAPTER TEN

IF WALLS COULD TALK

Not long after my wedding, my new husband paid off every remaining penny of my probation fees. With that, I was immediately discharged from probation, and my felony charge dissolved. My life was finally getting better—I was now a married, free woman!

But while I was "freed" from the State of Texas, a different kind of captivity awaited me.

Our first two years of marriage were incredible. We had all the elements of a thriving marriage—except for God. We attended church regularly and fully believed in Him, but God wasn't the foundation of our marriage. Soon enough, we'd see the results of that.

Both of us loved music, so we built an on-property studio and welcomed countless mainstream and local artists. I wrote and released various new projects, collaborating with well-known artists, swapping more features than I could count. I was Diamond, and everyone knew Diamond.

Before long, my influence spread throughout the region and eventually overflowed into neighboring states. My husband stood behind me

10,000%, supporting me in ways no one else ever had. I needed this; I needed him.

But, as we know, every influence has its own influence. By 2008, I began using marijuana. Everyone around me smoked weed—my friends, the artists booking sessions—it became an essential part of my life.

Before this, I'd never touched any kind of drug or tobacco. But soon enough, I became so dependent on weed that I could barely function without it. I needed to smoke to start my day, to eat, to write and record, even before intimacy. Everything became contingent on whether I'd smoked or not.

After two back-to-back car accidents in 2006, my body started feeling terrible every single day. A specialist confirmed that my back was seriously and irreparably damaged, with more issues than I was prepared to accept.

I started getting steroid injections to manage the pain, but before long, my doctor prescribed Oxycodone. Finally, I felt relief. I just wanted my regular life back.

At 26, my body often felt like it was sixty. My dependency and addiction to prescription pain medication gradually intensified.

Though I was never a drinker, two very powerful substances had taken over my life, and I couldn't function without either of them. This would go on for years.

Still, life continued. I stayed active and high-functioning, eventually deciding to pursue a career in cosmetology. I enrolled in school for hair and nails, and as usual, I did well academically.

During that time, I became good friends with my instructor, LaNeishia. Over the years, our friendship blossomed, and she would become incredibly instrumental in my life.

This was my girl! (And she still is to this day.) I could talk to her about anything, and she would listen. When challenges came, she was there. When we needed a girls' night or a getaway, she was there. I adored her.

As difficulties began surfacing in my marriage, I knew who to call. Although I've always kept my life's details private, I had three very close friends whom I entrusted with my most private moments, LaNeishia being one of them.

Like every marriage, ours went through storms. Most of the time, we worked through whatever came our way. But despite having three trustworthy friends, I started feeling like my life was unraveling. And not only that—I felt alone.

I hadn't felt this way in so long; I thought I'd left all of this behind. Though I poured into my children and my marriage, everything within me continued to crumble.

By 2009, my husband and I were more at odds than at peace. I wanted him to make me feel different, to meet my emotional needs. I deserved that. And slowly, everything from my past started creeping back in.

I started feeling angry, unheard, shut out, and unappreciated. As I stewed in those thoughts, the emotional waters rose higher and higher.

Certain things became enormous factors affecting my marriage, and I could feel depression settling in like an unwelcome guest. I was trapped— trapped in my mind, trapped in my emotions, trapped in my very existence. I poured myself into music, hoping it would release the pressure, but nothing seemed to help. Worse, everyone on the outside thought my life was perfect, and that enraged me. Nobody knew the battles I was fighting. No one knew my demons like I did. Now, I felt forced to keep up appearances, to be perfect because everyone expected me to be.

Later that year, after giving everything I had to this relationship, I sat front row as my marriage started to dissolve. I was tired of asking, tired of begging. Every plea began turning into resentment. I'd never struggled to be wanted in my adult life—never. Now, my spirit was vexed. I felt like he'd done so much to win me over, only to become complacent.

That was it! He was too comfortable. While I didn't want to sabotage my marriage as I had with past relationships, I had to do something to communicate my position and make my feelings known.

Sometimes, I'd leave for a day or two, and he'd immediately respond the way I wanted. I'd always been good at playing games; it was a control factor, something I'd mastered over time.

But eventually, even that tactic stopped working. My husband was smart and instinctive. I had to stay two steps ahead of him. Finally, after so many battles in our marriage, I reached my breaking point. I was leaving. I refused to keep feeling the way I had for so long.

I started packing my things and my children's belongings. If he wouldn't fight for our marriage, then neither would I.

With immediately essential items packed and taken to storage, I'd finally made my point. Marriage is a 360-degree commitment, and I wanted him to know that. Ironically, in pointing out all his faults, I'd managed to overlook my own. *Faults? What faults?* Oh, right—the imperfections that everyone else had, while I was free of them. Yeah, those.

Sure, I was a great wife in many ways. But I'd missed the fact that no man wants to listen to his wife complain day in and day out, to feel dishonored, disrespected, or unappreciated, or to be talked over by a woman who doesn't know when to close her mouth. I overlooked all of that. Nevertheless, I'd made my move, and I was sticking to it.

Alone in the quiet of my mother's home, the familiar lies crept in: "He doesn't want you." "He doesn't love you." "He doesn't appreciate you." "You're not enough." And in that moment, I believed every single one. It didn't matter that every day, my husband provided for his family, was a phenomenal father, never laid a hand on me, made sure I had everything I'd asked for physically, supported my dreams, and was faithful as far as I could prove. None of that counted. He was the complete opposite of the first man I'd married, yet here I was, still dissatisfied. Granted, he was prideful, arrogant, and stubborn, and certainly had some questionable occurrences, but he was still an exceptional husband.

They say hindsight is 20/20, but when we let selfishness and unyielding pride dictate our actions, we often miss the mark. I had been looking to my husband to give me a sense of completeness and fulfillment that only God could provide. I had wanted something from him that he was incapable of giving me.

After several short-lived exits, this time, I was serious—and I'd soon learn he was too. Settling in, away from home, I quickly realized my husband's stance wasn't budging. I didn't know how to feel, being used to him always urging me back. Not this time. I don't know who was coaching him, but whoever it was clearly knew a thing or two about collapsing marriages.

One week passed, then two, with minimal and strained contact. As time went on, our anger and bitterness grew. By the end of a month, I knew this wasn't going to end well.

I began planning to secure my own place, realizing that going home was becoming unrealistic. I was hurt, but I was also prideful. Why couldn't he just see that I was unfulfilled emotionally and fix it? It could've been so simple. While there were other factors, if he'd just met my emotional needs, things might have been different.

As more time slipped away, I could sense something happening behind the scenes. Anxiety and worry became my constant companions. Unknown to me, my suspicions were already confirmed.

I've never been the type to check phones, emails, texts, locations, or drive by houses. That always felt tacky and insecure to me. But this time, my intuition was on high alert. Something kept telling me, "Go by your house." And that's exactly what I did.

What I found there would turn out to be one of the most excruciating, disturbing moments of my life.

CHAPTER ELEVEN

SHATTERING VOWS

As I arrived in front of my home, I noticed a car parked there that didn't belong to either of us. Fighting to keep my composure, I knew. I knew there was a woman inside my home, with my husband.

To this day, I can't fully capture the emotion I felt in that moment. I died inside. Every trauma, every painful memory, every ounce of rage flooded over me. How could he do this to me? Every step I'd taken toward healing felt instantly undone. For the first time in my life, I wanted to physically harm someone. When I say I lost it, I mean I lost it.

This was my karma. Finally, I'd feel the same anguish I'd once caused someone else at seventeen. I felt the compounded pain of every heart I had broken, magnified a hundredfold. In more ways than one, I let him know that I knew. The next day, I hand delivered divorce papers to him. "Get 'em signed," I demanded. Without a word, he gently closed the door.

In the days that followed, we argued like never before. I could not believe he had brought this cheap, degraded, worthless whore of a woman into my home, onto the furniture I'd purchased. Even in my anger, I found I couldn't accept a loss without a fight. The dog in me just wouldn't let me do it.

As I sat in the wreckage of my life, I started to realize that everything I felt toward this woman was exactly what others had felt toward me for all those years. I was disgusted—with her, with him, and most of all, with myself. My mental health unraveled. I became completely non-functional. I honestly don't remember if my kids were with my mom or my sister during this time. I don't remember anything except being alive, locked in the hurt and rage that consumed me.

I know my godbrother Chris was around, but I don't actually remember his presence. Time drifted away in a fog. Uncertain of how much time had passed, what I do vividly recall was being at my sister's home one day, alone. Hearing a knock on the door, I stood up. Not knowing who was on the other side, I opened the door. Just as I did so, my mother stepped in. All she could do was wrap her arms around me. I was a walking corpse. She stood there, her arms squeezed tightly around me, holding on as if she never wanted to let go—as if an eternity could pass, and it still wouldn't be enough. When she finally let go, she sat to talk to me.

"Meka, you cannot live like this." At that point, I didn't care. I didn't want to live. This was the ultimate betrayal, and I was shattered beyond repair. Tears ran down my face as she held me and continued. "Baby, I understand. I know you're hurt, but your babies need you. You're not eating, you're not sleeping, you're not functioning. You have to get help, because if you don't, you're going to die." She begged me, her face filled with worry. "You're strong, you're resilient and you'll get through this."

Later that day, I took her advice and made a phone call. When the woman on the other end answered, I said softly, "I need to be seen." She asked why I needed the appointment, but I couldn't find the words. Where would I start? How much time did she have? What symptoms should I even mention? I had no idea. I didn't want to be labeled as depressed, suicidal, or crazy. I simply repeated, "I just need to be seen." I think she felt my urgency, because she quickly offered the next available slot.

Somehow, I managed to make it to the appointment the following morning. How I got there, only God knows. As I sat with my doctor in complete honesty, making him privy to the details of my anguish, I saw his face grow serious. He recommended a course of treatment and wrote me a prescription. I left, prescription in hand.

Back at my sister's apartment, I sank into the couch, opened the prescription bag, and pulled out the information sheet. As I read through the side effects and warnings, I thought, *Nothing could be worse than what was already happening.* I had no other options. I didn't want to talk to anyone; I couldn't pray. I was fading fast.

The doctor had said it could take a week to feel the effects. *Great. Another week of wanting to die.* I wrestled with my hesitation, but finally told myself, *Just take it.*

I opened the bottle, poured a pill into my hand, tossed it into the back of my mouth, and washed it down with a sip of Dr. Pepper. That pill would begin the deadliest chapter of my life—my life on Xanax.

Shortly after taking it, I felt drowsy, and before I knew it, I was fast asleep, locked in a heavy, dreamless slumber. It was the first time I'd truly rested in weeks. Hours later, I was jolted awake by loud pounding on the door. I sat up, heart racing, trying to process whether the pounding was real or a dream. I felt groggy, almost weak.

The pounding continued. I forced myself up, opened the door, and saw my mother, her face plagued with worry.

"Are you okay?" she asked. "I've called you a hundred times, and you didn't answer!" Her voice trembled as she continued, "The school called—they said you didn't pick up the girls."

In that moment, I understood why she was so panicked. I had never missed picking up my kids. She thought I had done something to myself. Although she never said it, I knew that fear had brought her here. She had even left my daughters in the car—something she never would've done under normal circumstances.

"I was asleep," I told her, explaining that the medication had knocked me out. I'd slept for at least eight hours. Relieved, she went back to the car to get my daughters. I think she thought keeping them there would help anchor me and invoke my usual parental functionality.

I guess she was right in a way. I sluggishly hugged the girls and asked them how their day was. Not knowing how sick their mommy truly was, they happily shared the details of their day and asked about mine. As I so often did, I shuffled my little white lie to the forefront. "Mommy's day was amazing" I quickly responded as my mom sat there with her head down.

She had already picked up food for the girls, so I got them ready for their baths. She stayed a while longer, then hesitated at the door before asking, "Are you going to be okay here with them?"

"Yes, Mom, we'll be fine," I assured her. She didn't leave until my sister and nephew arrived, finally feeling secure enough to go home. That night was the closest to normalcy I'd felt in a very long time.

In the days that followed, I began to adjust. Mentally, I could tell the medication was helping. Emotionally, though, I was still barely holding on. But for the first time, I felt the faintest sliver of hope that I could make it through this.

CHAPTER TWELVE

THE FATAL ANTIDOTE

As my mental and physical strength gradually returned, I felt ready to move the girls and myself into our own home. Though my husband and I were still at odds, I was finally able to think, sleep, and eat a bit. Even so, my weight kept dropping—I was down to 134 pounds, which felt alarmingly small for me.

At that time, I was working as a licensed private investigator, which gave me plenty of distractions. Diving into the tangled lives of others—pastors, wives, ex-husbands—allowed me to put some distance between myself and my own turmoil. Once settled into our new home, I found myself alone most of the time. The girls were at school during the day, and in my line of work, I was usually working solo.

While the medication was stabilizing me, I still felt emotionally fragile. Over the next few weeks, as I spent more time alone, my mind started shifting, trying to regain some semblance of control over my life.

By this time, my husband had ended his very short-lived extramarital fling. Though he'd moved on, things were only just beginning for me. My old habits, my anger, and my resentment were there, waiting patiently to resurface. In my brokenness, I knew these emotions would always show up for me. And, just like old friends, I welcomed them in.

As my pain began to recede, my anger amplified. Now, I hated her, I thought I hated my husband, and I hated everyone who had ever hurt me. I refused to be caught in the storm this time—I'd be the one unleashing it.

If you've followed my story this far, you know that there was never a deed that remained unsettled with me. This situation was no different; if anything, it heightened my sense of retribution. I reconnected with a few people from my past, even entertained some new acquaintances. My ex-situation, the one I'd hurriedly pushed out of my life for Dubb, was thrilled to hear about my separation. He and Dubb had a bitter, long-standing rivalry, having clashed and threatened each other more times than I could count. Their animosity fit perfectly into position.

While Dubb and I were speaking civilly, we were far from reconciling. He was still hurting from my departure, and I was still enraged by his actions. I loved him, but my resentment burned hotter.

For the next few months, Dubb and I lived separately. Still nurturing my well-worn, vengeful mindset, I decided to let my last ex visit. By now, Dubb knew where I was living, as we kept our relationships with our children intact. He was the only father the girls really knew, aside from a rare visit from their biological dad, and I was certainly the only mother my son had ever known. I was mindful of Dubb knowing where we lived, but at that point, I didn't care too much.

I hadn't been involved with anyone sexually since the separation, and truthfully, it was the last thing on my mind. Today was no different.

When my ex-fling arrived, he complimented the decor. "I see you haven't lost your touch. This place looks good… and so do you." I rolled my eyes, my tone sarcastic. "I know." He looked at me, puzzled. "What's wrong with you? I just got here."

I could barely mask my irritation. *Yeah, you just got here, and you were just leaving. Don't get too comfortable,* I thought.

"Nothing. You're just stating the obvious," I replied. He scratched his head. "Ooooh, here we go." I stood there with my arms folded, giving him my best rested poker face.

"Come over here; I'm not gonna bite you." He sounded almost pleading. I switched gears. "You want a drink?" He declined, and the room filled with awkward silence. I thought, *What am I even doing?* SMH.

A few minutes passed, and my mind raced. *How did he even pull me before? He's definitely not my type… I hope he doesn't think he's getting none… Man, I hope Dubb doesn't pull up.* Dubb had a habit of showing up unexpectedly, and if he found his archnemesis here, it would definitely make the news.

He tried to make small talk, but I wasn't interested. "What time do you have work tomorrow?" I asked, clearly signaling I was ready for him to go. He laughed, sensing my impatience. "You ready for me to leave already?" Yes, yes, I was. I smiled politely. "Just asking."

We exchanged a few more words, and he finally stood, as if ready to head out. I walked him toward the door, but he grabbed my wrist. "You know you're the best I ever had, right?" I knew it, but I didn't care to hear it. "I know," I said flatly. I wasn't desperate; I was acrimonious.

Almost reflexively, he dropped to his knees in front of me. "Uuuuh-uhhh… no, sir. Get up." He looked up, "Tamika…"

I immediately cut him off. "No. Really, get up." I wasn't after sex; I was after vindication. I wanted the chess move, to know I delt the last card and held the deck. But this wasn't the person, nor the method, I wanted to use.

Finally, I said, "I think you should leave." He complied.

While I had taken steps forward, I still didn't feel like myself. By now, I had created problem after problem. I was taking Xanax three times a day, smoking weed, and using Oxycodone. I was a beautiful, self-destructing shell of a woman.

My husband and I had postponed our divorce and started talking about reconciliation. Despite everything, we still loved each other, but there was so much unresolved tension between us. Dubb's pride was hurt by my leaving, and my heart was shattered. I was fragile, and so was our relationship. But he wanted his family back, and I thought I wanted that too—or so I told myself.

The day came when I agreed to move back home. We decided to set aside our differences and try to mend our broken marriage. But the more I sat within those walls, the more I regretted my choice. I couldn't step anywhere in my house without feeling the presence of another woman, who had dared to parade around in my home. No matter how brief her presence, it made me sick.

Though my husband was remorseful and took ownership of his actions, I found no relief. He often listed all the ways she had failed to measure up to me, but I didn't care. I no longer trusted him, and my resentment only deepened. I became colder and more vengeful than ever.

I shut God out completely. I felt unworthy of prayer and undeserving of healing. I no longer expected my marriage to survive. There was nothing anyone could do.

I longed to feel numb. Completely numb to everything around me. I craved an escape from every stimulus life offered.

I sank deeper and deeper into depression. I'd have brief bursts of energy, only to be blindsided by despair. Later, I learned I was suffering from manic depression and anxiety, with constant worry over things I couldn't control.

My self-worth was gone. I felt ugly, overweight, and, above all, unhappy. I barely felt like a wife or mother, yet somehow, I went through the motions.

Meanwhile, my husband did everything he could to make amends and help me feel secure. We still argued, but I often started it, constantly revisiting the pain of what he'd done.

He assured me he was mine, showing his commitment in every way he knew how. He got a full-body tattoo of me as a sleeve, inked his wedding ring, my name over his heart, a piece on his upper back dedicated to me, and even matching chess pieces with me later. But to me, it was just ink. Ink fades.

What didn't fade was the trauma I was carrying, from early childhood into my adulthood, woven deep within me, visible to no one but me. No matter how much I tried to quiet them, my suicidal thoughts returned with a vengeance.

To everyone on the outside, I had the perfect life—a great husband, beauty, talent, amazing kids, financial stability. They couldn't have been more wrong.

CHAPTER THIRTEEN

NOWHERE TO HIDE

By mid-2010, the walls finally collapsed, and everything I'd been holding in flooded out.

One day, I found myself behind the wheel of my Navigator, coming completely unglued. I was a wreck. I sped down Highway 80, driving erratically, tears streaming down my face as I completely unraveled. Then I noticed a State Trooper behind me, and of course, he pulled me over.

This felt like my moment. I always kept my handgun on me; while I had a permit, I often didn't carry it concealed. As he approached, I wrestled with countless scenarios in my mind—none that would harm him, but all with the hope that, in some way, I might be freed from my turmoil. Before I could make any choice, he was at my window.

I rolled it down and saw immediate compassion in his face. "Ma'am, I'm Texas State Trooper Davis. Are you alright?"

I couldn't find words. I hadn't taken any drugs—illegal or prescription— but I was a broken, silent storm. He asked again, "Ma'am, are you okay?" That did it; I crumbled.

"No," I managed to say through my tears, "no, I am not okay." He asked me to tell him what was wrong. "Everything," I replied. "Absolutely everything."

I poured out the darkest corners of my life to a complete stranger, and somehow, a small comfort seeped in. No one had asked if I was okay in such a long time. My family checked in, of course, but they never asked if I was *okay* in this way. I'd been conditioned to respond, "I'm fine, how are you?" instead of revealing any truth. But in this raw moment, I felt a tiny release.

This was my first, very brief flicker of peace. It wouldn't solve my problems, but it was a moment of reprieve. Following protocol, the trooper called a Crisis Intervention Advocate, and within minutes, they arrived. Though I was grateful for their presence, I knew that no advocate could help me—I needed *The* Advocate.

And just like always, my mother came. Her spirit lifted me in ways I couldn't lift myself, and this day was no different. She made sure I got home safe, likely carrying the weight of my suffering with her. I hated that my family was continually dragged into my chaos. I knew I had to isolate my struggles from them somehow.

I began to lean more on drugs to numb my pain and minimize my family's involvement. By 2012, a new chapter was finally opening—we were purchasing a new home. For the first time in years, I felt relief. I could live in a space free from the reminders that had haunted me in the old house. We even donated all the furniture to the family moving in; I wanted a fresh start and believed this could finally initiate my healing.

But as the saying goes, "No matter where you go, you're always there with you." I was about to learn that firsthand.

At first, everything seemed promising as we settled into the new home. Though my burdens were still very real, I was optimistic. We transitioned smoothly, but I had a scab I couldn't resist picking at. Some might call it self-sabotage; I saw it as refusing to let unresolved issues control my life. Either way, I craved closure.

My husband and I had a small disagreement, one that, for some reason, I couldn't let go of. After years together, I knew when he was lying, and while I sensed he was trying to protect me, it felt like an insult to my intelligence. I hated that he was withholding the truth, manipulating my response by hiding behind half-truths.

The argument simmered for days, a small fire waiting to catch a gust of wind. And when the wind came, so did the flames. There was only one issue causing this disconnect between us, but it was massive. I wanted to work through it, and he wasn't going to take that away from me. So, I stored the incident away in my mental files.

On the outside, my husband and I shared a decent life. We argued here and there, but we also shared countless perfect moments. We were, by all appearances, a great match. The problem was what we didn't show others—the weight I bore alone in silence. Determined to keep my issues from spilling over to my family, I resolved to keep them locked within.

Alone, I clawed through the darkness in my mind. I hid my tears from my children, crying only in secret spaces: the shower, solitary drives. This became my routine for years, numbing myself with Xanax and sleep.

By then, I'd managed to give up marijuana. I didn't like the grip it had over me; I wanted control, or at least the illusion of it. But in exchange, I turned to higher doses of Xanax. My family no longer smelled weed, but they saw something far more dangerous: I was slipping away. Mixing Xanax, muscle relaxers, and Oxycodone was a perfect recipe for a quiet, deadly escape.

In the midst of this, I lost a close family friend to a fatal Xanax overdose. It should have been my wake-up call. It wasn't.

The more my thoughts surfaced, the more I struggled to conceal them. I started sleeping even more, finding comfort only in oblivion. Sleep was the only place I didn't feel—no awareness, no pain, just a hollow shell.

Unseen by me, my husband had stepped in for our children. He filled in my blanks, showing up for them at school functions and events, all the times I was absent. He never said a word but silently fought for them and me. There are times I don't remember being there, but he was.

I tried to maintain some semblance of normalcy. I cooked, cleaned, and kept myself up—at least on the surface, doing what I could just to *be*. But I was damaged, out of touch with reality, an embarrassment to my family. I'd truly become the black sheep I never wanted to be.

At family functions, I'd show up so intoxicated that relatives would nudge me awake or tell me to go lie down. I was tearing my life apart in every possible way.

Anger, unforgiveness, bitterness, and resentment—they swallowed the very essence of my life. The woman I wanted to be was slipping away, leaving only a shadow.

Within the next year, crucial changes began to unfold that would completely alter the course of my life.

Originally, my primary care physician had prescribed my first dosage of Xanax, but I had since transferred my care to my local family doctor. He was an older gentleman—meek, kind-hearted, and passive. After years of seeing him, we'd established a comfortable rapport. I had always known my body well, and he trusted that. I could sneeze and accurately gauge what was wrong with me. I would walk into his office, tell him my symptoms, and he'd write my prescriptions based solely on that, without much question.

Most of my issues were routine, usually centered around seasonal allergies or minor illnesses. The only exception was my Xanax prescription. Over time, I had increased my own dosage from three times a day to four. While I knew he meant well, he never questioned my requests. This continued for longer than I could remember.

One day, however, he told me, out of the blue, that he'd soon be retiring. I hated to see him go, but I was happy he could finally enjoy his later years. Little did I know that his departure would bring my entire world crashing down.

When he retired, all his patients were referred out, including me. At my next scheduled appointment, I met my new doctor and went in expecting a routine visit for a refill.

As we reviewed my medical history, I noticed a sudden shift in his expression, as if he'd just seen a ghost. After a pause, he turned to me and cautiously asked, "Mrs. Dalton, with all due respect, are you selling your Xanax?"

"What? No! Why would I sell my Xanax?" I replied, completely shocked.

"Are you telling me that you—a five-foot-two, 160-pound woman—are actually taking this dosage of Xanax?" he asked, his disbelief evident.

"Uh… yeah?" I responded, still confused.

"No way," he said, shaking his head. "Do you realize there are men twice your size who can't tolerate this dosage? Little lady, you're lucky to be alive, and there is no way, absolutely no way, I would feel comfortable refilling this prescription."

Was he serious? More than serious. I realized then that the look on his face was one of genuine alarm. I was, in a sense, a walking ghost, completely unaware of the danger I was in. I later came to understand that my previous doctor's retirement had unexpectedly played a crucial role in saving my life.

I left his office fuming, but deep down, I knew he was right. He offered a non-narcotic alternative, which I refused, yet something inside me recognized that I needed help.

What was I supposed to do now with all these unresolved thoughts I could no longer numb away? I didn't know, but I would soon find out. Bracing myself, I sensed that all hell was about to break loose. Anyone who has struggled with addiction knows that the mere idea of losing access to your vice can be deeply unsettling.

Without the Xanax, my suppressed emotions began to surface, and sleep became nearly impossible. I developed insomnia, a cruel irony as I was already emotionally drained. I tried to hold myself together, but soon I was on a fast track to complete unraveling. Every unresolved issue from my past began flooding back, consuming my mind and igniting old rage.

The obsessive thoughts over the closure I craved consumed me. I knew my husband had lied to me, and I refused to let it go until I heard the truth from his mouth. As fate would have it, the opportunity presented itself: the woman who had disrupted my life wanted to talk, and I was ready to listen. While I would not soon get the truth directly from his mouth, I was more than willing to take the next best thing.

Our conversation lasted over an hour. I finally received answers to every question that had haunted me, every truth my husband had obscured or twisted over the years. Now, I had all the information I needed.

I kept it to myself, saying nothing. He never suspected that I had spoken with her, and I'm sure he would never have imagined it. But minute by minute, I meticulously plotted my revenge. How could he do this to me? How could he choose her over his commitment to me and our marriage instead of simply rising to the occasion?

The fact that he had lied to my face, time and again, filled me with a seething rage that went beyond simple hurt. This was anger on a level I'd never experienced—a simmering, calculated fury. I became like a predator, calm and patient, waiting for the perfect moment to strike.

A strange calmness settled over me, a sign that my resentment had come full circle. I was no longer in anguish; I was resolved, consumed with a need for retribution that left me feeling more focused than ever.

CHAPTER FOURTEEN

SNAPPED

Several days passed, and I finally invited my husband to sit with me. His face showed annoyance; he clearly thought this conversation would be like every other, where he could safely dismiss my questions. No matter what I thought I knew, he could always brush it off, and he had done so for years. He would lie, and there was nothing I could do to make him tell the truth. Even now, I can hear his arrogant tone as he'd always challenge me, "Prove it."

Today, though, we'd both get what we'd demanded. I was getting my truth, and he was getting his proof.

As with every other conversation, I lead with, "Is there anything you want to tell me?"

"No," he replied quickly.

"You sure about that?"

"Yep... I'm sure. What's up?" he said, with his usual cocky abrasiveness.

I kept my composure. "You tell me, honey. How about you use this time to tell me the truth about all the lies you've fed me for the past six years?"

"I'm not doing this dumb **** with you today!" he snapped. "I've already told you the truth."

Calmly, and unfazed, I responded, "That's fine. You just missed your final opportunity." He didn't seem to care. He clearly felt this was a casual rendition of all the times before.

I could have worked through the truth, but the lies... all those little white lies—I refused to accept.

With his dismissive and agitated tone, he replied, "What else?"

"I thought you'd never ask," I said, my unwavering glare searing through him, the tension hanging thick in the air. Watching his profuse anxiety build, I followed through. "I had a long, informative conversation with your little girlfriend, and you, Mr. Dalton, have most definitely been lying to me."

For the first time, he froze. Panic flickered across his face. "What are you talking about?" he demanded.

"Oh, I think you know exactly what I'm talking about. You've insulted my intelligence, played in my face, and tried to make me think I was delusional all this time. You've rebuilt this entire marriage on lies, and you most definitely have me five strokes past f'd up today."

In a measured, condescending tone, I started listing everything I knew she couldn't have made up—all the details that didn't align with his version of events.

The truth exploded between us, shattering whatever pretense we had left.

Oh, it definitely hit the fan, and it splattered on every wall in that house.

Caught completely off guard, he quickly rose for a heated argument, and without reservation, I gladly joined him. I would get my satisfaction today.

We hurled obscenities, each word like gasoline on a fire. I had given so much to this man, to our marriage—I had compromised in ways I could hardly admit to myself, sacrifices that gnawed at me daily. And this was how he repaid me? Absolutely not.

As the argument escalated, I felt something dark come over me. Before I could say "go", I attacked him. Just as my children's father had once done to me, I now became the aggressor. I didn't recognize myself. Who was I? What had I become?

All the bottled-up pain, every tear I'd shed, finally erupted into something unrecognizable. The gentle, nurturing spirit I once had was gone, replaced by someone fierce and relentless. The monster had been unleashed.

In that moment, I became the uncaring, heartless person I'd been so many years ago. I'd spent so much time trying to be everything he wanted me to be. Now, if he wanted a liar, I'd be that too. If he wanted a wife, I'd play that role. Nothing in me reflected who God called me to be; I was walking a dark path.

I'd handed every corner of my mind over to bitterness and resentment, giving the enemy unrestricted access to orchestrate my life. And like a twisted symphony, I played the keys.

From this point on, all bets were off. I'd returned to my old ways without a second thought. This road would only get darker.

CHAPTER FIFTEEN

THE DEPTHS OF REVENGE

Looking for ways to escape home, I found myself drawn to a privately governed organization. I had never been one for parties or crowds, but soon after initiating my prospecting period I caught the attention of a high-ranking player within this group.

Just like that, ol' faithful Jezebel was back. Old habits came rushing back. I could feel his intense interest in the way he spoke to me, the way his gaze lingered on me, and the special treatment he subtly offered. His physical traits reminded me of an ex, but I effortlessly disregarded the resemblance—as irony would have it, he had his own connection to a past relationship by default, one I won't unpack here, but let's just say there was definitely someone we had in common, and it wasn't just me.

As usual, I played my hand with charm and intrigue. We spent hours talking on the phone, and soon he was bringing me flowers and lunch at work. He showered me with attention, which was thrilling, but for me, it was more than that. This was about the strategy; it was the ultimate chess move.

Before long, I was letting him and other "brothers and sisters" from the organization into my home to celebrate my induction, knowing very well our involvement, a very spiteful vindictive move. My husband was there, of course. At first, it wasn't a problem, but that didn't last. He knew me too well—he sensed something had changed. And I wanted him to.

Complicating things further, my new "fix" already had a live-in, long-term situation with another member closely tied to us both. I didn't care. If I wanted someone, I didn't think twice about who they "belonged" to. To this day, I'm not sure if I was really drawn to his mind and dominance as I'd thought, but we connected regardless. The relationship quickly became physical, escalating faster than anything I'd experienced before. On at least two occasions, he proposed to me. But in my mind, I never intended it to go that far.

For me, controlling another man was always effortless, but this was bigger than control. This was my way of balancing the scales, of hurting my husband as he'd hurt me. At the same time, this man was growing on me. His "girlfriend" was furious with me, but I continued to make demands, and he met every one. When I requested a new CLS 550 Mercedes and he handed it over without hesitation, I knew I had him. I made it clear that even though I was married, he was my man. Both he and my husband belonged to me.

This brought my husband and me to a breaking point, as you might expect.

At that point, I didn't see the downside. I was already as hurt as I could possibly be—nothing could top the betrayal I'd already experienced. With that in mind, we separated. I refused to let the new man go, especially not because my husband demanded it. How dare he make demands of me? This was my game, my rules.

For months, I held my ground. On multiple occasions, my husband and I clashed over the other man being in "our" home. Suddenly it was a problem? How convenient. I calmly brushed off his threats and anger. If ever there was a "couldn't care less" attitude, it was mine.

For over a year, I paraded around with the "other man," but as we always did, Dubb and I eventually reconciled, only to fall back into the same cycle. While I loved him, the resentment I carried was so deep that vengeance was the only response I knew. No matter what I did to even the score, nothing truly satisfied my need. I kept digging myself deeper into sin, but nothing brought the resolution I craved. Nothing stopped the bleeding.

By this point, I was a fully functional, beautiful, and meticulously tidy liar. I had somehow become everything I had despised in others.

"He who buries an axe carries a torch," and I was living proof.

CHAPTER SIXTEEN

UNCHARTED TERRITORY

Harboring all my hurt, a tainted spirit, and the broken pieces of my life had finally reached a breaking point. One day, I found myself overwhelmed by anger and defeat, simply too exhausted to keep fighting. I wanted it all to be over. This time, I was ready to move on.

After weeks of consideration, I concluded it was time to cut ties and take my losses. I was tired of reliving past traumas, trapped by thoughts of lies and regrets. I wanted to be free.

Calmly, I started packing my things and my daughters' belongings. I no longer wanted my home, the possessions within, or even my marriage. Without prior notice, with no indication of where I was headed, I left. I let go of all the emotions that had haunted me for years. I walked away from everything.

Surprisingly, the girls and I adjusted seamlessly. For them, their acceptance likely stemmed from the fact that they were still seeing their dad and brother regularly. They were probably as tired as I was of all the endless conflict. While I needed room to breathe and realign, I think my husband did too. In a strange, compassionate way, I knew he deserved better, and wanted him to have it.

I knew he was a phenomenal man, a wonderful father, and a devoted husband, but I couldn't get past the battle in my mind. Yes, he could be manipulative and controlling, but evidently, so could I. And somehow, his faults weighed heavier on me than my own.

So, I stuck to my decision: I would not go back "home."

With newfound freedom, I had plenty of time to think, to be alone. Though I was still emotionally displaced, I felt some relief; the weight that had once consumed my mind no longer felt as overpowering. Looking back, perhaps it was because, in a way, I had allowed the enemy to win. I had handed over my marriage, tied up with a pretty red bow. There was no more struggle in that regard, but the fight was far from over.

With my divorce filed and awaiting finalization, I began to flirt here and there, nothing beyond innocent exchanges. A few caught my interest, and one man became a particular prospect, but his background wasn't a good match. Ironically, I still wasn't seeking God as I should have; instead, I misappropriated this opportunity for true change.

As I quickly rose to the top of the "Most Eligible Bachelorette" list, I found myself filtering out suitors, dodging the undesirables, and being especially picky about who I'd let into my space. I knew what I wanted in a man: God-fearing, tall, handsome, intellectual, ambitious, a great father, attentive, loving, respected, and willing to spoil me. Looking back, I realized I had that in front of me all along. Not one of the people I entertained could come close.

As time passed, I still had zero interest in anyone. I even encouraged Dubb to date, though he sternly refused each time. I thought he would change his mind eventually. I was wrong.

One of my greatest challenges was that I was an overthinker. People approached me daily, but I knew there were always hidden agendas. I was well-known, commonly referenced as a local celebrity—affluent, business-minded, successful, smart, and attractive. I knew they saw me as a "trophy," a "come-up." I was familiar with the approach. I'd utilized it on countless occasions, but I refused to be anyone's stepping stone.

In the end, I stayed low-key, inaccessible, and enjoyed my privacy. I had always kept my intimate dealings mostly under wraps, earning me a reputation as someone untouchable and hard to reach—which, in reality, was true. My standards were high, and I was determined to keep them that way.

So, I avoided anyone who knew me or knew of me; that was too easy. Instead, I began talking to a man from Baton Rouge. I loved men from Louisiana—their accents, their confidence. In all honesty, I hadn't anticipated anything serious; I just wanted someone to help pass the time.

Since I'd had no plans of reconciling with Dubb, I didn't see myself in any real commitment. But, of course, the man from Baton Rouge became relevant. Although he wasn't exactly my "type," his conversation was engaging, and his sexual appeal quickly became an issue. What started as a way to pass the time turned into something more, a lot more.

When he asked about my ex, I was upfront with him for once. I told him Dubb was extremely non-negotiable when it came to me. Anyone who knew Dubb knew what that meant. While we had indeed had our ups and downs, it was always up when it came down to me and his approach towards anyone I was dealing with. Although we were finalizing our divorce, Dubb's protective nature towards my "potentials" had not diminished.

The new man, however, wasn't fazed. He was well-acquainted with all walks of life, and his calm, composed demeanor masked a level of intensity I hadn't anticipated.

Over the next several months, I was transparent with both Dubb and the new man. They each knew about the other. Although I understood the history Dubb and I shared, I thought we were done.

We kept things civil enough for the kids to go back and forth between our homes, but I knew this wasn't sustainable. As things escalated, I found myself bouncing between the two, trying to manage their tempers in one chaotic episode after another.

I remember my hairstylist used to joke, "Just tell me what color you want me to wear, 'cause Dubb is gonna kill you," after witnessing some of the incidents firsthand.

At one point, I told them both, "This has turned into full-time adult daycare." It was exhausting, yet somehow, something began to shift. After over a decade of begging Dubb to want me the way I wanted to be wanted, he finally did.

I'd always liked my man a little "crazy" about me, and now, I had that—times two. It was a compromise of peace, to say the least.

Eventually, this situation spiraled so far out of control that I realized the only way to restore order was to leave. And that's exactly what I did, moving far, far away.

After my divorce was finalized, I moved five hours away, hoping for a fresh start. While the intensity of my old ways had dulled somewhat, I was still deeply entangled with both Dubb and Q. (Deep sigh) I didn't know why I was like this. Dubb and I had been through so much that he felt like a part of me, but at the same time, I couldn't seem to peel myself away from Q, even though we had almost nothing in common.

By this point, Dubb and Q had come close to killing each other at least three times—literally. My feelings for Dubb were tangled with unresolved emotions and anger, yet he stayed through it all. Even after everything, he continued to care for the girls and me, treating us as if we were still under the same roof. Occasionally, we were intimate, and despite our separation, he still felt like my husband. Somehow, it was as if he had wanted me to move on, yet couldn't fully let go. No matter what, he stayed through every moment of it, while not peacefully, he stayed, none the less.

Meanwhile, I couldn't trust Q. He was sneaky, skilled at concealing whatever he was up to. Looking back, I don't even think we liked each other, but the intoxicating pull between us sexually was undeniable. It felt like an addiction. I prayed countless times for God to break the hold he had over me, but it only seemed to strengthen. Despite all the red flags, I kept going back to him.

I knew he had to be sent from hell, yet I continued my dealings with him.

I recall so many times praying for God to sever my addiction to him, because that's exactly what it had become—a very unhealthy, unsolidified soul tie. And it went both ways. He was as heavily addicted to me as I was to him.

I tried everything to separate myself, even watching Juanita Bynum's *No More Sheets* sermon on multiple occasions. No matter what I did, our sexual bond only strengthened. While I wasn't addicted to sex, I was unquestionably addicted to sex with him.

Our connection was intense but hollow. I disliked so many things about him. As an only child, he was spoiled, passive, and dependent, relying on others to cater to him—traits I couldn't respect. He cared only about two things: sex and basketball. Every time I expressed my "non-negotiables," he would change temporarily, just long enough to stay in my life. He knew I was infamous for cutting people off and understood that if he "dropped the ball," Dubb would be right there, ready to rebound and score.

While Q loved me, I never treated him with the care, respect, or priority I gave Dubb. I couldn't imagine putting Q first, given all the betrayal and mistrust between us, while my loyalty to Dubb lingered in the background. I knew my actions were unfair, but my connection with Dubb overpowered everything else.

Whenever holidays came around, I spent each one with Dubb and my immediate family, never offering even a split of time with Q. Crazy as it sounds, it was a routine I couldn't break. My life had become a circus, and I was desperate to find a way to bring the chaos to an end. My spirit yearned for peace, for God's presence.

While Q didn't live with us, he would drive five hours each way just to spend a few hours with me, often arriving unannounced. Other times, I'd sneak back into town with him, keeping it low-key. The craziness of it all was overwhelming, but he kept showing up.

One Sunday morning, trying to reconnect with God, I asked Q to come to church with us. Surprisingly, he agreed. Just as we stepped outside, Dubb showed up—five hours away from home and not for worship. "Sunday's Best" quickly devolved into "Hell's Kitchen."

Dubb had an uncanny ability to provoke Q, and Q, in turn, would retaliate in ways that he knew would drive Dubb over the edge. They were relentless in escalating each other's fury, both determined not to back down. Dubb might have let me carry on with Q, but there were always unspoken boundaries, and I knew I had to tread carefully. Although Dubb was passively dominant, he still commanded control, and I understood the rules.

Soon, all of this tension would ignite the perfect storm. While I'd seen hints of Q's temper before, I was about to find out just how dangerous he could be.

Arguments between us escalated with every new conflict. Though he was smaller in stature than most men I'd been with, he was dangerously strong and quiet—a lethal combination I had underestimated.

One night, after another of Dubb's unexpected appearances, Q was furious. Whether or not what Dubb had implied was true, just the idea of me being intimate with anyone else sent him into a frenzy.

Before I knew it, Q had straddled me, his hands gripped tightly around my throat. I could feel the air escaping as I struggled, vision blurring, every muscle in my body weakening. His face was inches from mine, his eyes dark and unflinching. I tried to gasp, but the pressure was relentless. I felt my ears pop, my nose block up, and stars burst in front of my eyes as a splitting headache set in. He wasn't letting go.

I tried to mouth the words, "I can't breathe," but he only leaned closer, tightening his grip. Glaring into my eyes, with the darkest, most chilling and intensely unbroken stare I'd ever seen, he began to verbalize his warning. "***** I will kill you. I will ******* kill you". Completely unmoved by my silent plea for help, I started to feel the pressure around my throat tighten. Leaning the weight of his upper body more closely to mine, and increasing the amount of weight against the clench of my throat, he softly pressed his lips against my left ear. In a very low, very calm tone he began to elaborate his prior statement. "If I find out you ******* this *****, both of y'all are dead". Abruptly snatching his hands from around my throat, he casually got up off of me and strolled into the living room like nothing had happened.

Still in shock, I lay there, too stunned to move. The calm he had displayed, the deadly control—this was not what I had seen before. This wasn't the chaotic rage I'd known from my past. This was something much darker, much more precise.

As I lay there, realizing the depth of the situation I'd walked into, I quickly realized I was in uncharted territory.

CHAPTER SEVENTEEN

A SLAVE TO SIN

Over time, I became accustomed to the intense, turbulent rhythm that defined my relationship with Q. It was a cycle of scandal, physical altercations (including one incident with a 9mm handgun), mutual provocation, and a constant undercurrent of toxicity. Cheating, lying, and threats became our normal, followed up by steamy, tension-fueled makeup sessions. Somehow, in this mess, we thrived off each other. There were moments that shattered me, that could have been life-altering, but we continued. As dysfunctional as it was, we "cared" for each other.

Q was, in a twisted way, what I'd needed to distract myself from the pain I felt with Dubb. And while Q pulled me into the depths of chaos, Dubb became more present in my life than ever before—attentive and protective, though often in ways I hadn't expected.

I was never truly afraid of Q himself; I was afraid of what he could do, of what Dubb could do, and eventually, of what I might do if pushed too far. The threats, the anger, and the potential for violence hung over us all. It was a precarious game, with stakes that grew higher each time they clashed. I knew that at any given time, Q could leverage the private details of our involvement and I would never be able to look my children, family, business associates, or anyone else in the face again.

After our most heated arguments, he would send me clips from our private moments, some of which I'd consented to, others I hadn't even known about. These videos were his insurance, his way of holding onto me. He knew how much I valued my privacy, my image. With each video he sent, he was passively reminding me of the control he held, forcing me to stay well within his boundary lines.

Dubb could sense that something deeper was holding me in place. "What does he have over you?" he'd ask, knowing it wasn't like me to be tethered to anyone in a way I couldn't break free from. For over a year, I told Dubb only a fraction of the truth. Yes, the pull I felt with Q was highly physical, but there was more. My fear of public exposure kept me trapped in a prison of my own making. I did not want the world having unrestricted access to my sexual exploitations.

As the mental strain grew unbearable, I decided to free myself from the prison of worrying that in one of Q's vindictive tantrums, he'd send our videos to Dubb as a way to damage anything he assumed I was rebuilding behind the scenes. I had reached a decision: I would take control of my secrets. I would tell Dubb the truth, not allowing Q the satisfaction of holding it over me anymore. If anyone was going to reveal these details, it would be me. One morning, I called Dubb and, after gauging his mood, decided it was now or never. "Wussup pretty girl" he welcomed in his usual salutation. I took a deep breath and began.

"Well, there's something I need to tell you," I said, keeping my voice steady.

"Oh yeah? What's that?", his tone shifting, as if he already knew this conversation wouldn't be easy.

"I want to clear up some things," I began. "There's more to why I've been unable to let Q go."

He paused, then answered calmly, "I'm listening."

I swallowed hard. "We have sex tapes. A lot. Some I knew about, but others I didn't. He has them all." I braced myself. "If we fall out, it's up."

Dubb let out a measured "Hmm." Then, he asked, "So, I take it you've seen these tapes?"

"Yes," I admitted.

"So, if they're in his possession, how'd you see them"? I'm sure trying to pinpoint our last time together.

"He sent me clips," I hurried to explain.

"Send them to me," he demanded, his voice level but firm.

"What? Why would I do that?" I was so thrown off guard. "I'm not doing that."

He repeated himself, unmoved. "Send them to me."

I wasn't prepared for his response. My mind scrambled. If I didn't send them, he'd think I was hiding something. But if I did, he could use them as ammunition against Q, igniting more conflict.

I needed time to think. I explained my discomfort, hoping he would understand. For the moment, he let it go, but I could tell it was far from over.

Dubb had always let things slide with me. It was almost as if he'd rather have me, even partially, than not at all. I'd never been sure if he felt this way because he was prepared to let me seek "justice" for the pain he'd caused, or if he was simply willing to wait.

Their rivalry was fierce, each unwilling to let the other "win." This demand from Dubb lingered in my mind, so I decided to be honest with Q as well and lay it all out. To my surprise, Q took it calmly, shrugging it off as if he didn't mind. "Send them to him, then," he said.

Although he realized that he had lost that leverage over me by way of surprising Dubb, in a sense, he still found gratification in knowing he knew.

For the first time in years, I felt free. The truth, that elusive, powerful thing I had avoided, was finally out in the open. It no longer held me captive. This weight lifted from my shoulders. There was nothing left for Q to hold over me.

Several conversations with Dubb followed, but he never reacted with anger. In fact, he seemed oddly accepting, and I realized how deeply we understood each other's flaws. But seeing those videos laid bare the truth of how lost I'd been, how much I'd let myself be controlled. For the first time, I saw the depths of my captivity. And I knew I was done.

Though Q and I remained entangled for a few more months, after more than three years, I began to detach. I became painfully aware of the hurt my actions could bring to Dubb, no matter how "strong" he was. Slowly, my desire for Q started to dwindle, and he sensed it too. I realized that while Q had helped me bury my pain with Dubb, I was only trading one problem for another, piling hurt on top of hurt, dragging my soul further into turmoil.

Eventually, I visited Q one last time. The experience was empty. I was over it. As I headed to my car, I looked him in the eyes and said, "Q, I'm done." And I was. After years of entanglement, I stopped calling, texting, or answering him. It would be years before we spoke again. For the first time, I stood my ground—and I walked away.

CHAPTER EIGHTEEN

PRISONER OF PERCEPTION

The decision to cut Q off weighed on me for quite some time, but soon my focus shifted. Details about my family dynamics and background that I had once taken as unshakable truths would soon be challenged, providing all the distraction I needed. One after the next, gut-wrenching revelations began quietly stepping into the spotlight of my life.

One day, out of nowhere, I found myself on the phone with my older sister. We didn't speak often, but whenever we did, it felt as if no time had passed; we'd catch up on every corner of our lives. This time, I was venting about my mother, frustrated with emotions I was sorting through and feeling deeply abandoned. I felt cast out, like the "black sheep," and couldn't shake the anger bubbling inside me—not because she was a bad mother, but because it seemed that, in all the chaotic and reckless decisions I'd made in my life, she hadn't come to my aid the way she had for my two other sisters. I'd watched her offer them support, just as I believed my grandmother had done for her. Now, in the middle of one of the most uncertain storms of my life, unrelated to anything discussed here, there I was—no call back, no advice, no follow-up, no support system.

Looking back now, I realize I needed that space. God was building something stronger within me, but in the moment, all I could feel was fury. I launched into a passionate tirade, listing the countless selfless acts I had done for my family, friends, strangers—everyone. I'd given my time, energy, and even money, freely and without expecting anything in return. My heart had always been compassionate, and I'd never asked for anything back. But on this day, my isolation was affixed solely to what others had not done for me.

I knew Biblically that when you publicize helping others, it taints the blessing itself and can cut off your own. But this wasn't that, right? This was me venting about the irony and audacity that the same generosity I'd given freely had not been returned. Mind you, this wasn't even a conversation about money! Somehow in the midst of my frustration I had overlooked all the times that my mother had been there for me.

As I finally came to a pause, my sister replied, calmly but firmly. "Meka, you know I understand. I get it, but just because you are 'you' to others doesn't mean others will be 'you' to you. One thing I can clear up, though, is this: as long as you allow unforgiveness, bitterness, and anger to control you, it will. And it will consume you."

Her words hit me hard. I hadn't expected that to be her response, but it was exactly what I needed to hear. This was what I had done my entire life: let resentment take root. And in that moment, I realized how much I had allowed it to define my relationships. It was a pre-lightbulb moment, though I wasn't yet ready to fully embrace it.

But as always, just when I thought I had managed to push the issue aside, the enemy returned with the one thing he knew always struck a nerve—

abandonment. In some form, this feeling always found its way back to me. My grandmother, whom I knew always intended well, had created an emotional distance between my mother and me. She'd often remind me with a phrase she never strayed too far from: "She might'a had you, but I'm your momma." My older sister and I would sit quietly, listening as our grandmother recounted all that she had done for us—specifically, my sister and me. At some point, I came to see that everything she had intended to make known was not only clear but deeply embedded in me. That simple statement weakened me in a way I couldn't yet articulate.

Not long after the conversation regarding my mom, I found myself needing to request a copy of my birth certificate for some reason—I don't even remember what for. As I glanced down to verify the information, I froze. I had always known, even from a young age, that my grandmother had legally adopted both me and my older sister. It wasn't a secret; I'd heard it my whole life. But seeing my grandmother's name listed as my mother, with no entry at all for "father," broke something inside me. In that moment, I felt utterly worthless, nameless even.

Suddenly, everything I had been trying to work through in relation to my mother compounded and intensified, and it only got worse from there. As I always did, I bottled up those feelings, closing the lid tightly over them, letting the emotions simmer in silence.

No sooner than I began to hear the metal lid spinning closed around the glass mason jar of my emotions, I began receiving third-party messages from family members and missed calls from a Houston number I didn't recognize. My irritation mounted. The number belonged to none other than my older sister's father, a man I had known of but never truly known. Out of nowhere, "congratulations" started pouring in from him. My grandmother, during one of her usual gossip sessions with her longtime acquaintance and ex-son-in-law, had apparently been updating him on my music career and hinting at the success she saw in my near future.

I tried to be polite, but something in me recoiled at his sudden interest. Why was he so urgent to be one of the first to congratulate me? Of course, I knew who he was in general terms, but before this, he had never reached out. In an instant, I concluded he had an ulterior motive.

As time went on, his calls became more frequent. Anyone who truly knows me knows I despise being on the phone, especially with people I don't know. Three minutes or less is usually my max. But one day, he called and led with the usual small talk, asking about my music and the girls. I responded politely, thinking nothing of it, until he abruptly said, "I always knew you were my daughter."

"What?" I stammered. "What did you just say?"

Without hesitation, he repeated the exact same words. Shock washed over me, and I slowly lowered the phone from my ear, staring at the screen while he continued speaking. I could hear his voice, but it was like my mind stopped processing English.

Many years ago, this theory had been tossed around lightly, but I'd never given it much thought. I remembered one specific instance in 2006 when I was livid with my entire family for arranging a way for him to see my children against my wishes.

Desperate to end the call, I remember him telling me, "Don't call me back on this number. I'll call you when I'm by myself." By now, he was remarried and actively parenting his other children.

I sat there, silent, unable to believe what I'd just heard. This man couldn't possibly be my father. I had already lost and grieved my father at fifteen. This man couldn't be my father—at least, he'd better not be, because if he was, I was sure I'd develop a hatred for him that I'd never known. What kind of man leaves a child fatherless, knowing he's the father, and only reaches out when she's approaching success? And worse, he would keep me hidden from his current family, like some test tube accident from some type of donation clinic? He had to be out of his entire mind. No way! Absolutely not!

The news was too much to stomach. I wanted answers, but I already had enough confusion in my life. If this was true, it meant my entire life had been built on a lie. My identity, my history, everything I'd experienced was drenched in deception.

Seemingly, all areas of my existence appeared to be wrapped in layers of lies, not just my own, but those carried in the quiet, hidden hands of my family. Secrets whispered; truths twisted—my world was steeped in deception. My God, I'd been a terrible person at times, making mistakes I couldn't deny, but did I truly deserve this? This weight of betrayal, the unearthing of secrets I'd never even imagined? Surely not.

CHAPTER NINETEEN

WHAT DOESN'T KILL YOU

I clung to my emotions, refusing to jump to conclusions I couldn't handle. In that moment, everything simply was what it was—or wasn't. The past was out of my reach; I could only shape what lay ahead. Yet, as my sister had warned, bitterness was taking root. It consumed me—my thoughts, my emotions, my actions, even my reactions.

Determined not to let it win, I began the hard work of building a mental environment where I could release the pain and confusion. Much of the chaos I lived in was my own creation, but I realized something powerful: while external circumstances might contribute to my struggles, they didn't have to define me.

I began to understand that contributing factors are not determining factors. The power to change lay within me.

For too long, I had been living on autopilot, letting my emotions be dictated by what others brought into my life. That wasn't living—it was surviving in the shadows of others' choices. I was absorbing the residue of someone else's actions, mixing it with my own pain, and letting it poison me. Everything around me dictated what happened within me.

But as I faced this truth, I began to feel a shift—like a slow chisel breaking away the invisible chains that had bound me for so long. Something had to change. And by something, I meant everything.

Slowly, I stopped trying to control everything around me and began focusing on something far more important: controlling what was within me—self-control. For the first time, I wanted to truly live—not just for my children or my family, but for myself. I wanted to step into the life God had created me for.

I didn't know what full surrender to God looked like yet—I wouldn't for a while—but I knew this was the first step.

Piece by piece, I began the long and ongoing process of unpacking the traumas of my life. I realized that to step into my future, I had to stop clinging to my past. What I hadn't understood before was that much of what I was experiencing wasn't even mine to carry. So much of it was tied to the trauma and cycles of others.

Though I had studied psychology and pursued a career in forensic psychology, I quickly realized the human heart couldn't be understood through textbook theories. People's struggles weren't just psychological; they were deeply spiritual.

I was committed to understanding the "why" behind people's actions, but I knew this had to start with me.

As I unmasked my circumstances, I stood face-to-faith—yes, faith—with everything I had felt. Day by day, emotion by emotion, I confronted them.

At the top of my list was alone.

For much of my life, despite what others might have seen as resilience, strength, or perfection, I had felt deeply, painfully alone. If I had felt this way, surely others had too.

And then it clicked. Like the sun breaking through storm clouds, I realized God had allowed everything I'd endured for a purpose far greater than myself. In that moment, I knew He wanted me to serve others.

First, I turned my focus to the man I knew, deep in my soul, that God had chosen for me. Our past was a tangled mess—a battlefield of mistakes, wounds, and unspoken shame I had carried like dead weight for far too long. But I was ready to shed it all. I knew I couldn't move forward without first walking through the fire of truth.

With trembling hands and a heart full of uncertainty, I laid everything bare. I shared every detail—every hidden moment, every misstep, every painful truth I had kept locked away in the shadows of my guilt. It was raw, uncomfortable, and terrifying, but I refused to hold anything back. For years, I had allowed the weight of secrecy to press down on my spirit. That day, I chose to release it all.

As the words spilled from my mouth, I braced for the worst—for rejection, anger, or the heartbreak of seeing his love waver. But instead, something unexpected happened. With each truth I revealed, I felt a heaviness lift. The walls I had built around my heart began to crumble. I could almost feel the grip of the enemy weakening with every honest admission.

It was then that I realized something profound: the enemy cannot survive in the presence of truth. Lies are his stronghold, but truth is God's domain. By exposing the darkness within me to the light, I stripped the enemy of his power. And in that vulnerable moment, I saw God's hand moving—not to destroy, but to restore.

To my amazement, the man before me did not shrink away. He listened, unwavering, his love unshaken. He met my vulnerability not with judgment but with grace, a reflection of God's forgiveness. I realized that sharing my truth wasn't just an act of courage; it was an act of redemption. It wasn't just about unburdening myself; it was about inviting God to heal what had been broken.

That moment wasn't just about honesty—it was about liberation. It was about reclaiming the pieces of myself I had lost in the darkness. Truth didn't just set me free; it became the foundation upon which we could rebuild something stronger, something rooted in grace, understanding, and unyielding love. Together, we stepped into a new chapter, not defined by the mistakes of the past but by the redemptive power of truth and forgiveness.

I followed with my children, confronting the painful truth I had long avoided: the countless times I had fallen short, the moments I had failed them, the ways I had let them down. The weight of those realizations was crushing, but it propelled me to make a solemn vow—to become better. A better mother who nurtured without fail, a better friend who listened without judgment, and a better confidant who provided unwavering support. I knew I needed their forgiveness, and for the first time, I was fully prepared to humble myself and ask for it.

Then came my mother. She, too, deserved a better version of me—a better daughter.

For years, I had harbored anger and resentment toward her. I thought I understood her actions, but I didn't truly know her story. I hadn't known her brokenness, her pain, her struggles. I hadn't seen the manipulation and trauma she endured from her own family—including my grandmother—and from her own personal relationships in life.

I didn't know about the battles she fought to keep her children, only to have them torn away. I didn't understand the mental prison she lived in every day. Later, I would learn that my grandmother had endured many of the same struggles as well.

These revelations made me see why Satan is called an "ancient foe." Generation after generation, he uses the same tactics, destroying families with subtle lies and one ultimate goal: division.

This was why my sister had been so adamant about not leaving my children with my mother. Slowly, lesson after lesson unfolded before me like ancient scrolls.

And then something unimaginable happened: all the rage and unforgiveness I had carried for so long began to melt away.

Compassion took its place.

Every enemy in your life needs a place to hide. Sometimes it's in a dark closet, sometimes in other people, and sometimes in the shadowed corners of your own mind. It's the unseen enemy that catches you off guard.

We can prepare for the threats we can see with the naked eye, but it's the hidden ones—the unresolved wounds, the lies we tell ourselves—that overtake us. Living in darkness and hiding from the truth is like harboring a dangerous fugitive. Stop giving Satan a place to hide.

Although my journey and God's plan for my life hadn't yet come full circle, I committed to walking in the authority He had given me. And that journey began with one powerful step: forgiveness.

CHAPTER TWENTY

REDEMPTION

By 2019, most of my mistakes and struggles were finally behind me. I had committed to mentoring my first group of women, hoping to be someone they could trust, confide in, and look to for guidance along their own paths. My goal was to be the change I wished to see in the world and, even more, in myself. Fueled by a genuine passion for helping people find their own purpose and excellence, I committed to the well-being and growth of others and being used as God saw fit for their lives. The fulfillment that followed was beyond anything I had ever known.

After years of tearing down myself and, at times, others, and after struggling with career direction and my own self-worth, I finally found my calling. To my surprise, it had never been about fitting in but about standing out. I realized that I was not meant to follow but to lead—and to lead by example.

By this time, I had freed myself from every toxic relationship and unhealthy capacity I had been bound to. Though I was uncertain where my relationship with my true life partner would lead, I had found deep forgiveness, not only for myself but also for him, for the other woman, for my exes, for my family, and even for those who harbored resentment toward me. I was flourishing, and if I could see it, I knew God could too.

After a lifetime spent seeking acceptance, I finally understood that God's love for me was indescribable, unchanging, and never dependent on what people did or didn't do. I had also taken my sister's advice to heart. I began welcoming the potential family I had with my father and siblings, knowing that I'd already found my true Father, and His love for me would never fall apart, never not show up, and never fail me. Unaware of if we shared blood ties or not, I treated my potential family as if they were all my own; embracing them fully and letting go of the negative connotations attached to the past.

Amid my journey of growth, I received an unexpected email. I had completely forgotten about the Ancestry DNA test I had submitted. Though there was no direct connection to my sister's father, I did find enlightening new family ties.

At the top of the list were my mother and two siblings. My mother showed a 50% DNA match (and reflected as my mother). My baby sister (whom we have always known did not share a father with either of us) displayed a 25% DNA match and reflected as either a half-sister or a niece. My oldest sister showed a 45–52% DNA match and reflected as a full sibling, indicative of sharing both the same mother and father.

Seeing the confirmation, I felt neither elated nor disappointed. It simply was. I had an answer, and thanks to the work God was doing in my heart, I was ready to accept it as it was. I was more grateful for the change and posture of my heart than the finality of the genetic answer.

As I've reflected, it's not the outcomes that shape us but the lies, unforgiveness, rebellion, and uncertainties that can destroy us. We demand truth but often welcome lies. When we shut God out, we invite the enemy in. Jesus is the way, the truth, and the life, and without Him, we have no way to get to the truth that leads to that life that he designed for us.

Weighed down by shame, we carry condemnation, guilt, anger, unforgiveness, and countless other burdens that God sent His Son to free us from. Every day, we choose whether to settle into circumstances or live in God's promises. God's plans for each of us are unique. Mine is not yours, nor is yours mine. But God's purpose is real, for us and for future generations. Faith, commitment, and trusting God's timing lead us toward that purpose.

I had spent years looking in the mirror without truly seeing myself. Fixated on the world's opinions, I ignored what God saw in me. From an early age, I had unknowingly handed over control to the enemy. The deep-rooted issue in my life was in my heart, and I had been unaware of the damage I was causing myself.

I saved every hurtful memory as a justification to disobey God. I handed the keys of my life over to the enemy, allowing him to drive me toward destruction. My emotions governed my actions, my choices, and every consequence that came with them. I became my own worst enemy, convinced that my way would lead me to fulfillment. But it only deepened my emptiness.

The short-term gratification was fleeting. I couldn't see that in the moments when my life felt like it was unraveling, God was working to position each broken piece for His glory. But my anger, betrayal, and rejection blinded me to His purpose.

I realized that I had allowed the enemy into my life, not only through my choices but through my inability to forgive. Friendships, family, all of it—I was finally learning to let go, spending my time in environments that aligned with my purpose. There are as many people on my block list as on my prayer list. I have learned the power of praying for my enemies—not for punishment but for blessing. Praying for them frees me from anger and allows me to release the past fully.

Sharing the details of my life is not about pride in my decisions. It's about pride in the Father who redeems. My story is a beacon of hope for others walking the same path I once did. I was chosen, even in all my filth. God's grace, mercy, and forgiveness have brought me to this place.

The moment I began releasing my grip on the toxic influences that had been poisoning my life and traded them for a genuine pursuit of God, everything started to transform. The things I had once been so certain I wanted no longer held the same appeal. My desires shifted—no longer driven by self-gratification, fleeting fulfillment, or temporary emotional contentment.

Now, I wanted God. I craved His presence, His purpose, and the life He had always intended for me. When I gave Him unrestricted authority to move in my life, He began to pour out gifts that were pure, untainted, and everlasting. In that surrender, He revealed the true meaning of His promise to give me the desires of my heart.

But here's what I came to understand—He wasn't simply granting my old wishes. Instead, He was reshaping the very core of my desires. What I longed for now reflected His will, His plan, and His love for me. It was no longer about chasing what I thought would satisfy me. It was about aligning my heart with His purpose, and in doing so, everything began to change.

This alignment was more than a shift in perspective—it was a transformation of my soul. In seeking Him, I discovered that the things I desired were the very things He had always intended for my life, and that realization brought me a peace and fulfillment I never imagined possible.

In the fall of 2020, I remarried my soulmate, the man God had prepared for me. His patience, love, and unwavering support taught me the true meaning of forgiveness. Shortly before we remarried, I found a small yellow notepad filled with prayers he had written daily during our separation—prayers for my heart, our marriage, my healing, and my forgiveness. In that moment, I understood the true power of love.

Of all the trauma and negative experiences in my life, nothing in the world had impacted me as profoundly as love. In that moment, I discovered a truth that would forever shape my heart:

"Three things will last forever—faith, hope, and love—and the greatest of these is love." —1 Corinthians 13:13

Finally, I find myself in a position where I have truly learned the meaning of repentance, honor, long-suffering, and love. In every step of this journey, God has shown up for me without fail.

Additionally, my mother and I share a happy, healthy, and loving relationship for which I am more thankful for than 100 million breaths. There is truly no one on this earth like my mother. God, in His infinite wisdom, knew exactly what I needed as a daughter and in a mother. He perfectly signed His name into every fiber of her being.

On February 10, 2021, my grandmother passed away. While she didn't live to see the full fruition of her prayers, I know she would have been proud. I am thankful for all she instilled in me.

In 2022, my husband and I welcomed a beautiful baby girl and continue to watch our three older children thrive with God as their foundation. In June 2023, I launched Prestigious Prep University, a coaching and mentorship platform built for entrepreneurial education and dedicated to helping others find their purpose and inspire those around them.

In June 2024, through fasting and prayer, God revealed more of Himself to me. For the first time, I saw that I had been a professing "Christian" without fully living for God. Now, I'm able to hear Him clearly because I have prepared a clean atmosphere within me for His Holy Spirit to dwell. I am learning that it's not just what we say but what we do that truly represents Him. Not long after, I was delivered from the things that had silently remained hidden in the background uninterrupted. In full repentance, I rededicated my life to God and was baptized alongside my oldest daughter not long after.

At 42, I know just how close God is to the brokenhearted. Though I have no control over what may come, I can share my testimony to encourage others to take that leap of faith. A life without God is as bad as it can get.

On Sunday, November 17, 2024, as I neared the completion of this book, I attended my church and heard my pastor, Dr. Ed Newton, begin his second sermon in his sermon series, "The Kingdom of God." His words brought a flood of tears as I realized, with complete certainty, that God had confirmed my purpose in writing this book. Every experience, every struggle, and every victory was for this moment—to help others, to glorify Him, and to serve as a testament to His unfailing love.

With each word Pastor Newton spoke, I felt a profound sense of affirmation. God was speaking through him, showing me that my journey—all the heartbreak, lessons, and redemption—wasn't just for me. It was a testimony, a beacon for others lost in their own battles, looking for light.

Every reservation I had regarding not wanting to share the details of my life gently faded away. Thank you, Pastor Ed, for always sharing God's calling for your life in a way that teaches and leads others to serve just as Jesus did. I encourage you to listen to this very same sermon. The sermon can be viewed at:
https://www.youtube.com/live/e3mb1RwDEp4?feature=shared

November 18, 2024, on my original anniversary date, I completed my first book, *Black Sheep, White Lies.*

I pray this blesses your life in the midst of every storm and in every moment of peace and healing that follows.

I invite you, right now, in the eye of your storm, to surrender it all to God: your life, your circumstances, your pain, and your destiny.

If you are ready to surrender to the Almighty, living God, pray these words with sincerity, conviction, and a will to transform and walk into everything He has called you to be.

Lord Jesus, I know I'm not perfect. I'm a sinner, but I believe in You. I believe that You sent Your only Son to die for my sins, that I may have life, and have it more abundantly. I desire to live the life that You have called me to live. Save me. Change me. I give You my life.

If you have prayed this prayer in faith, God has seen your heart and heard your cry. Rise up and walk in victory! Remember that serving God and surrendering to His will does not exempt us from life's challenges or the possibility of things falling apart. The difference is that in serving and trusting God, He will take care of you in ways you can't imagine, providing assurance and peace that, no matter how difficult things may seem or feel, He is working it all out for your ultimate good.

If no one has ever told you, or you just haven't heard it often enough: I am proud of you, and CONGRATULATIONS! I CELEBRATE YOUR LIFE AND ALL THAT IT HAS TO OFFER, NOT JUST FOR YOURSELF, BUT IN THE LIVES OF OTHERS, FOR THE GLORY OF GOD. YOU MADE IT!

INTERVENTION – RESOURCES – ADVOCATES

If you are battling thoughts of suicide, there's help.

Please reach out to the **Suicide & Crisis Lifeline** by dialing **988**. You'll be connected with a live, trained crisis counselor who can provide immediate support. This is a nationwide and confidential service.

Are you or someone you know a victim of domestic violence?

You are not alone. There's help. Your safety is sacred.

Please call the **National Domestic Violence Hotline** at **1-800-799-SAFE (7233)** or text **"START" to 88788**. Trained advocates are available to provide confidential assistance, crisis intervention, and referrals to local resources.

Do you just want or need someone to pray with or for you?

There's always someone willing to listen.

The **Billy Graham Evangelistic Association Prayer Line** is available at **1-888-388-2683**. Trained volunteers provide spiritual support and prayer, offering comfort and guidance grounded in Christian faith.

Are you struggling with addiction and need help turning your life around?

You're just a call away from the first step toward change.

Contact the **Substance Abuse and Mental Health Services Administration (SAMHSA)** at **1-800-662-HELP (4357)**. This confidential, free service provides information and referrals for individuals facing substance use disorders, connecting you with local treatment facilities, support groups, and community-based organizations.

If your situation is an immediate, life-threatening emergency, PLEASE CALL 911 IMMEDIATELY.